PURITY MAKES THE HEART GROW STRONGER

Purity Makes the Heart Grow Stronger
Sexuality and the Single Christian

Julia Duin

VINE
BOOKS
Servant Publications
Ann Arbor, Michigan

7303

Vine Books is an imprint of Servant Publications especially
designed to serve Evangelical Christians.

Published by Servant Books
P.O. Box 8617
Ann Arbor, Michigan 48107

"A Celibate Epiphany" is reprinted from *The Sighting* by Luci
Shaw by permission of Harold Shaw Publishers, Wheaton,
Illinois. Copyright © 1981 by Luci Shaw.

Printed in the United States of America
ISBN 0-89283-373-4
88 89 90 91 92   10 9 8 7 6 5 4 3 2 1

Library of Congress Cataloging-in-Publication Data

Duin, Julia.
    Purity makes the heart grow stronger: sexuality and the
single Christian / Julia Duin.
        p. cm.
    ISBN 0-89283-373-4
    1. Chastity. 2. Single people—Religious life. 3. Christian
life—1960 I. Title.
BV4647.C5D78   1988
248.84—dc19   88-1586
                                                    CIP

*Dedicated to eight single men and
women ir my life:
Kevin, Karin, Cheri, David,
Lorna, Tom, James, and Brother Gregory
without whose encouragement and advice
I would have never dared begin this book.*

Table of Contents

Introduction

THIS BOOK GREW OUT OF a conversation I had several years ago with an editor of *Christianity Today*. I was frustrated over the dearth of believable literature on how single Christians should handle their sexuality. Much of what I had seen was written by religious professionals, doctors, counselors, theologians, and pastors who were hardly typical of the secular mind set that most of us face at school and at work.

As a religion reporter for the *Houston Chronicle*, the largest daily newspaper in the Southwest outside of Los Angeles, I see much of what goes on in the secular as well as the religious worlds. Sometimes it is hard to tell the two apart. Other times, it seems as though the religious world is truly on another planet as far as sexuality is concerned. In many newsrooms, as well as other work places, conversations revolve around sexual matters. It is expected that we can intelligently discuss them. In the church, we act as though sex does not exist. Much material on the subject from a religious point of view either sets no standards or is written too dispassionately, as if the authors never had a moment of sexual desire. Sexuality is not a surgical procedure; it is in the fiber of our being. Yet, the secular assumption that living out one's sexuality means having sex is echoed by many evangelical Christians. Single people are not thought of as having sexual potential until about two months before marriage, when they are deluged with Christian sex manuals.

But Jesus, whom we worship, was the most balanced person this world will ever see. Yet he never had sex. And neither will many of us, if I rightly perceive the direction of the tides of the times. I, who am in the latter part of the baby boom, am part of the increasing number of people in my generation who are staying single and not marrying. More of these single people are female than male, and in the last few years, a rash of secular articles and books have been published on the talented female who cannot find a mate. This problem is especially acute among evangelical Christian women in the baby boom who vastly outnumber available Christian men. And no one seems all that concerned about the fact that a large disenfranchised group of people is growing old in the church.

I cannot buffer the pain that many single people feel as they see their chances for a sexual relationship within marriage slip away with the years. I would like to help them face reality by coming to terms with their sexuality before their biological clocks run out and bitterness sets in. We do have a chance to witness to the world by our insistence on sexual purity. One major stand Christians can take that will make people stop and take notice of us is our refusal to indulge in the casual sex that our secular generation considers to be a moral right.

My conversation with the editor led to a column in the March 26, 1986 *Christianity Today* titled "Celibrating Celibacy." The piece drew many letters and long-distance phone calls and inquiries from three publishers. Having recently moved from Miami, I was only five months into my first year at the *Chronicle* when I agreed to write this book in early 1987. I'd ordinarily advise no one to try this task during their first year on a demanding job. Yet, I felt the time was ripe. When the PTL scandals broke a month later, I knew I had made a wise choice.

I don't claim to have all the answers on sexuality for single Christians. Any reporter knows there are two sides to every story, and it is while listening to both sides that I am sometimes torn. If there is no biblical directive on a given subject, I fall back on my own experience. I don't claim infallibility for my conclusions, but they are my best shot at speaking to those singles of my generation who struggle to live out their faith in the marketplace from someone who is in the marketplace herself.

Houston
November, 1987

ONE

Going against the Culture

O N ONE OF SOUTHEAST TEXAS' WARM, moist May mornings when the sun hung limp in a pale, languid sky, I was on the fifth floor of the *Chronicle* building in downtown Houston, carving up a rich chocolate birthday cake. We reporters and editors, a mixed barrel of people whose common ground was a love of writing and a desk in the *Chronicle*'s features department, were discussing the almost daily revelations of yet another sex-and-religion scandal that pockmarked the spring of 1987. Never, we all agreed while gulping down cake and coffee, had we seen anything quite like it.

Were there, someone asked, any new revelations on the wires that day? I showed them a *Detroit Free Press* cartoon pasted by my door of two wide-eyed parents and their child in front of a TV while a newscaster said, "And now, before we do religious news, we urge all children to leave the room . . ."

Everyone within earshot laughed because recently every major religion story, except the upcoming papal visit, was related in some way to illicit sex. First, it was the Episcopalians: the Diocese of Newark, New Jersey suggested in January 1987 that it could be time for the church to bless sexual relationships between the widowed, the divorced, the never-married, and homosexuals. Around the same time, a well-known ex-gay Christian leader resigned his post with a Christian group because of sexual involvements. In February, we wrote about a local pastor forced out of his church because of adultery. The

PTL story broke in March and continued for the rest of the year. In May, the leader of a nationally known college ministry resigned because of adultery. The same month, we broke the story on a Texas Methodist bishop whose death from AIDS was connected with a homosexual lifestyle. Not to mention never-ending wire stories on priests with AIDS, homosexuals in the ministry, and women having affairs with Roman Catholic clergy. Then in February 1988, televangelist Jimmy Swaggart was exposed for sexual indiscretions. After Gary Hart dropped out of the presidential race over his alleged sexual liaisons, one commentator quipped, "Well, it's about time we got sex out of religion and back into politics where it belongs."

It felt like a flood. The Christian press and various spokesmen wavered between defensiveness and disgust at each new revelation of yet another Christian leader involved in sexual sin. Many religious leaders blamed us, the secular press, for reporting on it. Others blamed themselves, for after all, the news was finally out that despite all those biblical passages on sex and related topics, Christians differed little from unbelievers on giving free reign to their sexual desires.

All this only reinforced my prior conviction that Christians generally are not told how to handle sexual desires intelligently. These desires are seen as okay for the married couple but forbidden for the unmarried who are left alone to figure out how to control these longings that inhabit our beings. Certainly we learned during that newsworthy spring that Christians can sin just as spectacularly as everyone else; what made it more odious to the non-believer was the pretense of virtue, which is why everyone gleefully jumped on former PTL hosts Jim and Tammy Bakker. Those of us covering religion in the secular press know of other religion scandals that remain uncovered that we cannot prove or print. So, skepticism reigns as to whether anyone is really sexually pure.

Abstinence from sex is still considered a rarity. Some people can't imagine this state of being. I remember working several years ago under an editor who was a real terror. She had derision down to a fine art. She directed me to write a story on weekend leisure activities in South Florida. I couldn't dredge up a decent lead sentence until I remembered some of the great Sunday brunches and Friday night pizzas I had eaten. Voila! I typed out a sentence to the effect of "Tired after a long week, South Florida residents' first thought upon arriving home from work is what they can find in the refrigerator." I sent the editor the story via computer.

After reading it, she shot me a look reminiscent of the last Ice Age, then tapped out a few editing suggestions. When the story showed back up on my computer screen, the instructions were to redo the lead. "What most people think about on Friday nights," she noted, "is how they can have sex."

For those of us for whom casual sex is not an option, there remains the problem of just what else to fix our minds on. Colossians 3:2 says to get our minds on things above, which is no easy feat. We get a lot of input from things below. Although you may not guess it from conversations in most church fellowship halls, the average single Christian is quite sexually knowledgeable. It is impossible not to be since we live in a society where newspapers carry sex surveys in their Living sections and news anchors on late-night newscasts detail the deviant sexual practices that lead to AIDS. Even an innocent shopping trip to the supermarket takes us past magazines touting such articles as, "Sexual Surprises: Which Men are Best in Bed?" "Smarter, Safer Birth Control" and "The Enticement of Lingerie."

Many of our friends consider life without sex abnormal. If we are divorced or widowed, they wonder why we don't use our newfound freedom to explore sexual frontiers; if we used to sleep around before conversion but now do not, people wonder why we are acting virtuous all of a sudden. Virginity is rarely mentioned except during references to the Virgin Mary at Christmas. It is literally a joke the rest of the year, like the time I picked up a greeting card that read on the outside,

"Many years ago, people remained pure, chaste, and whole-some and were called virgins. Today, some people still remain pure, chaste, and wholesome . . ." and the inside punchline, "They are called lepers."

Even though AIDS and related diseases have made sexual abstinence more the fashion at present, peoples' motives for not having sex now stem more from fear than conviction. "The safest sex would appear to be chaste sex," Colorado Episcopal Bishop William Frey wrote in the *Rocky Mountain News.* "And, in the words of one member of the British Parliament, 'Fear of death may succeed where quiet moral persuasion has failed,'" he added.

Our culture is not enamored with chastity in or outside of marriage, chastity meaning faithfulness within marriage and abstinence from sex outside of marriage. This is different from celibacy, which means permanent abstinence from sex. Society instead expects that everyone needs and wants sex. The unmarried are portrayed as sexually active on most TV sitcoms. Sex between the unmarried is considered normal, accepted, and fashionable. Why else would the federal government, knowing that everyone won't heed its instructions to stay celibate outside of marriage, suggest the practice of "safe sex?" Only 20 percent of all unmarried women in their twenties are still virgins, according to numerous surveys, including a 1983 study paid for by the National Institute of Health in Bethesda, Maryland. One-third of all single women in their twenties, about 2.4 million people, have lived with a man at some point, the study said. The poll takers didn't seek men's reactions. They might have found that not all men are hopelessly engulfed by lust. Some male friends tell me they are also willing to remain virgins until their wedding day, in spite of overwhelming peer pressures to have sex to prove their manhood.

Everything tells us that the chaste among us are out of step. I was at a luncheon where the speaker was describing his forty-fifth birthday. "Up until now," he said, "my two main interests in life were sex and sex. Now they're politics and religion."

Everyone laughed. I felt completely out of touch. If my two interests in life consisted of sex and more sex, I'd be in trouble. If nothing else, chastity does force one to develop more wide-ranging interests.

Yet, the sexual revolution awaits a coroner's report while we Christians have the opportunity of presenting another view of sex, a perspective smeared unfortunately by various religion-and-sex scandals. The world may know that Christians sin, but do they know how we avoid sin? Do Christians know? Do we care?

When people need a place somewhere for support, some head for a bar. We as believers in Christ should head for a church. However, in most congregations virtue is assumed but not taught. Christian books abound on sexual technique for married Christians, but little exists for the unmarried which is not simplistic and insulting to anyone of average intelligence and normal desires. After all, people reason, what is there to write about abstaining? Sex is seen as fulfillment; virginity as a vacuum. How many Sunday school classes really address this topic the way it should be addressed? Though there are classes on the family and on being happily married, I see little in the way of Abstinence 101. No, churches tend to expect singles to marry and assume that singleness and celibacy are only temporary. And woe to us if it is permanent. One single male friend of mine often complains that what riles him on this matter aren't the unbelievers, but the believers. He once wrote, "What gets to me is the incessant barrage of questions like, 'Are you married?' or 'How old did you say you were?' or 'Oh, you've never been married?' or 'Didn't it work out?' *ad nauseam.*"

Not finding comfort in a church, some of us head for small groups. My biggest helpers here have been Christian couples who either have teenagers or college-age kids or who work with that age group as professionals. They at least understand how common sex before marriage is. But those people are rare.

It is very difficult for single Christians to mention their

sexual desires for fear of being thought unspiritual. However, those thoughts are never far from our minds. I was once part of a weekly women's Bible study group of four. Over breakfast one morning in a coffee shop, I timidly asked for prayer because I was approaching my thirtieth birthday and the wait, with no end in sight, was getting rougher and rougher. Their reaction was typical. Two of the three women were so busy fighting off their husbands' frequent requests for sex that the thought of single life in a double bed seemed heavenly to them. The third woman, who taught at a high school, was more understanding, but she did not know how to console me. Sometimes it is hard to listen to advice on self-control from the married because to us it is much like a fat man telling a thin man how to fast.

Failing to find support from other Christians, singles' last resorts are each other. Even this can be empty. I'm surprised on dates to find Christian men who don't hold the same hard and fast line that I do. One man told me that he couldn't see why sex couldn't take place before marriage, "if two people really loved each other," he explained, to which I replied that women often feel exploited in these cases. If the man really loved her, he would wait for her. But it struck me how much he, a professedly committed Christian, still believed that he had sexual options. The Lord gives us none.

I've always felt that chastity is a realistic standard. One of the hottest topics I covered at the 1987 Episcopal Diocese of Texas yearly convention was a resolution on chastity. The priest who proposed the resolution did so because he felt that people were confused with the crosscurrents of religious and secular thought on the subject and no longer knew what the church stood for. Another priest argued against the resolution—which later passed—by saying that it would pass judgment on all those single people who could not or would not be chaste, as if they didn't have it in them to be so. I felt like chucking my portable computer (Radio Shack terminals that reporters use on the road) at him. I wanted to shout out that self-control was possible: that I was managing it and so could others if they really wanted to.

C.S. Lewis says that we choose every day which direction we shall go in life: directions that lead either toward heaven or hell. Those choices never seem that portentous when first made, but they form an unmistakable path in one direction or the other as the years go by. One Christian reporter told me that the first few choices to abstain from premarital sex were the most difficult for him. But after he set a pattern of saying no, he grew more used to refusing. He hardened himself to teasing from people, seeing that as only hot air. Then someone tried to seduce him at a party. What made him fight her off instead of giving in were the prior choices he had made, which by now had become a pattern. He had invested so much in keeping his sexual purity, he told me, that he saw no reason to give it up on a whim.

But he began by making a choice. Our station in life is determined by choices, choices to work hard or slough off; choices to sacrifice for a lofty goal or satisfy the urge of the moment; the choice to persevere or give up. Once we break our pattern of right choices and lose our virginity, that pattern is broken. Our spiritual concentration is shattered and all motivation for maintaining purity vanishes out the window. It is true that although we can't regain our virginity, we can regain our chastity. All the same, that original purity is worth keeping.

We may not be able to have sex, but we can enjoy our sexuality. Sex and sexuality are two different things that the world fuses together, saying that to be a real man you must be good in bed; to be a real woman, you must experience orgasm.

That message comes at us from all sides. I was hammering out a story on a black Baptist group one afternoon when in walked a co-worker with two just-released paperbacks: Andrew Greely's latest book and a potboiler on a former nun. Surely, she said, I'd want to read them. I picked up the book on the nun, half-guessing its contents: a nun spends years fighting restrictions imposed by her order and finally leaves it, but not until the explosive scene near the end where she happily loses her virginity. Only then does she feel she has finally become a woman. It was such a predictable line: religion restricts but sex frees up. We only become adults when we have sex. And so on.

That's the stuff of fairy tales. We all know that sex doesn't bestow instant maturity, and I think the opposite can be true: premarital sex exposes our immaturity and inability to wait for the best.

Christ didn't need sex to be a man. Being a man involves courage, taking risk, leadership, decisiveness, tenderness, and gentleness as well. If we can't develop our sex lives, we can develop our femininity and masculinity. God, the creator of sex, created alternatives. We would do him justice to see what those alternatives are.

TWO

Chaste Does Not Make Waste

ASHING TO WORK ONE CHILLY APRIL morning, I was stopped dead in my tracks by the sight of the word "abstinence" on the *Chronicle*'s front page. Peering at the paper on the news stand, I read the headline, "Reagan says abstinence 'good answer' to AIDS." President Reagan, the article said, had agreed to fight AIDS to the tune of one billion dollars in federal funds, but he also insisted that moral values be taught along with sex education on AIDS. The "abstinence angle" popped up in another news story about Attorney General Edwin Meese, who stated that any health education materials published by the federal government must place sexuality within the context of marriage. That memo didn't go over so well among various public health officials and politicians, one of whom insisted that it left out many sexually active Americans. "It's quite obvious that chastity and monogamy are not uniformly practiced in this country," he noted.

At least the chaste lifestyle is acknowledged. Too bad it's not encouraged more. Typically, sexual activity, not the lack of it, makes good news fodder. In spite of government officials' support of abstinence, those who practice it are idealized in fantasy but scorned in reality. I used to have long conversations with a co-worker who sat near me in the newsroom. When work was at a lull, we'd discuss our weekends and what we liked

21

to do for fun. It came out that I spent an inordinate amount of time at church. When he asked why I didn't spend my weekends with men, it became plain that our sexual lives differed vastly. He seemingly slept with everyone and I slept with no one. He couldn't imagine that. Our conversations went like this:

He: "Julia, if you'd just relax a bit and sleep with someone, you'd be a lot more fun to be with."

I: "Why should I waste myself on some guy who'll sleep with someone else the next weekend? You've got to be kidding."

He: "I can't believe how uptight you are. You'd better face facts about life, girl. I don't know who you think you're waiting around for. Why don't you go out and live life for a change?"

I: "I am living life, pea brain. There are other things to get excited about besides sex."

He: "Like what? I'm the one who's open minded. You're the one who's closed minded. You need to experience things if you're going to be writing about what this world's really like. I feel sorry for your husband, whoever he'll be. If it's two virgins getting married, you'll have a rotten wedding night."

I: "Your concern is deeply touching. I think we'll do just swell and we'll be able to satisfy each other."

He: "What? Without rehearsing?"

He thinks like a lot of people I know. Their line is that you must be sexually active because that makes you more open, fun to be with, and better schooled about the world. When I disagreed and suggested that sex might not be the key to "having it all," I tossed his value system in the ocean. He replied with a threat: if I didn't do things his way, then the consummation of marriage would be miserable because of lack of expertise in bed.

The "awful wedding night" threat is a common one used in varying degrees by our sexually active friends either out of spite (some people genuinely detest sexual purity) or concern. Lack of sexual experience does not ruin a honeymoon. The only study I've found on this was published thirty years ago in the *American Sociological Review*. This 1958 study compared early marriage experiences of virgins to non-virgins, shooting holes in my friend's hypothesis that no sex before marriage makes a dull honeymoon. There in black and white were statistics that showed that virgins had more enjoyable honeymoons than did non-virgins. That's right. Out of 177 recently married women in the survey, 45 percent of them were not virgins when married, which is amazing considering that this was 1958, several years before the sexual revolution really took off. Seventy-one percent of the non-virgins said they had satisfying wedding nights compared to 47 percent of the virgins. As for the uncomfortable 53 percent of the virgins before marriage who reported experiencing sexual difficulties, their number sank to 24 percent by the end of two weeks. The study added other figures to show that non-virgins experienced the greater sexual difficulties during their honeymoons than did the virgins, perhaps because the non-virgins' expectations were higher. Also, the thoughts of previous sexual indiscretions by the non-virgins, also known as guilty consciences, were plaguing their marriages.

That reminded me of the night I was driving home from a church event when I asked a girlfriend how she felt about her various romances back in her twenties.

"I wish I had remained a virgin," she said sadly. "Now when I marry someone, I'll be comparing his technique to all the other men I've known. And I wish that weren't so. I wish I could start all over again fresh and new with no memories of past 'Great Performances.'"

People tend to compare their present sexual experiences to previous liaisons. How could you not? Forty-two percent of the women in the American Sociological Review survey said their premarital sex life did not benefit their married sex life because of other difficulties that arose. Thus, one may be able to blunt the shock of premier sexual contact on the wedding night through premarital sex, but the result is usually no short-cut to sexual bliss in marriage. Conversely, 14 percent of the non-virgins said that long-term difficulties in their marriages began during their honeymoons. The report concluded that despite numerous physical difficulties experienced on the wedding night, the virgins attained to a considerable amount of sexual adjustment in a short period of time.

We simply must stand up to friends, classmates, and co-workers who overtly or covertly insinuate that we should be having sex now. Often these are people who, having slept around considerably, recognize that they've lost their market value in the marriage game for unspoiled goods. To maximize their own status, they defame or deny virginity's existence. Virgins can expect constant put-downs from those who tell us how "narrow-minded," "strict," "frigid," and "closed" we are to hold out for sex within marriage. As we approach and enter our thirties, those voices will get shriller as they perceive our time is running out. Ignore them. A move made in desperation is no better than inaction. Recently, a married Christian colleague gave me some welcome advice: "Sex isn't everything in marriage," she said, "and I certainly wouldn't marry for the sake of it. Follow your instincts and wait for the right man."

Despite the prospect that AIDS and other sexual diseases may bring in the so-called "Straight Age," many people honestly feel that sexual abstinence is not possible. Sexual indulgence is considered nearly a moral right in our culture. A case in point is a 1986 United Press International story about how the "girl next door" image of virtuous beauties of the 1940s and 1950s like Donna Reed, Jane Powell, Janet Leigh, Doris Day, and Debbie Reynolds has been supplanted by the likes of Cyndi Lauper and Madonna. The former kinds of women wore Peter Pan collars, flared skirts, cardigan sweaters, saddle shoes, and a look of innocence. They put off sex until they married. Now the "girl next door" has become a loosely dressed swinger for whom virginity would be a nightmare.

For the non-swingers it can be awkward. When I lived in Miami, a single friend of mine from out of state asked to meet me for breakfast. She was a college friend who had surprised us all by going to law school. We met at a plush hotel by Biscayne Bay, she dressed in the kind of conservative blue suit that is supposed to mark up-and-coming lawyers. We were both twenty-nine. She told me of an incident at a thirtieth birthday party for another single friend. What disturbed her deeply was one of the birthday cards this friend got that said on the front that there are worse things than being over thirty. On the inside, the sentence concluded with, "You could still be a virgin."

I can still see the pain on the young lawyer's face. "I felt like a freak," she told me. I think many singles lose their virginity because they have no compelling reason not to do so. And they don't want to be considered freaks. While everything at school and what they read shouts 'yes!,' religious institutions say little. Young people are naturally modest—who can forget the agony of seventh-grade locker room days when everyone had to undress in front of everyone else in order to shower—and it takes a lot to tear those barriers down. But once breached, then comes the flood. Teens don't try sex once, then quit. No, surveys indicate that most keep coming back for more.

Teenagers will abstain from sex if they can find powerful enough reasons to do so. Even if we think the teenagers we know are ready to engage in sex any day, the number one priority should be getting them to commit their lives to Christ. It is true that once the Lord has an open door, the Holy Spirit can quickly put the brakes to a bad relationship, which he did in my junior year of high school. This involved a certain good-looking guy in my math class. A new Christian, I was presented with a possible romantic relationship with him. Had I pursued it, I might have gone quickly off course. Fortunately, I had a new set of Christian friends who advised me not to go out with a non-Christian man, but most teenagers don't have that kind of support.

A Christian commitment or upbringing is no guarantee against sin. Teens active in church are often just as sexually active as those outside of church. Many teens are bored in church, so they'll test authority by eating the forbidden fruit: sex. Girls see how they are the only ones in their crowd who are not on the Pill; the boys are running up the tab on who has made it with the most women. Christian teenagers who are not challenged at church will aim for the ultimate frontier that all their friends are trying. Sex is pervasive in youth culture and it's almost impossible for young people not to be obsessed with it. For them, sexual desire is new and strong and difficult to control. And many girls play at sexual flirtation because they are so innocent about how this affects men. That was certainly true when I was in junior high and wearing my skirts as short as they would go. I—and most of my friends—were totally oblivious as to how we came across.

The logical conclusion to our youth culture is death: either through alcohol, drugs, suicides, or auto accidents by which youth are killing themselves off. They see the world is a lie and that they can't escape the depression that involvement in sex and disobedience to God brings. If they don't die, then their consciences are seared by frequent sin through sexual immorality, rebellion against authority, and heavy use of drugs and alcohol. Most have a rough time believing such behavior is bad and they don't perceive evil for what it truly is. They are casual about sin. The church, which is the major if not only setter of moral standards in their lives, rarely presents alternatives to what the world has to offer.

What the church can offer them is the cross. I've found that youth have a natural inclination to accept difficult challenges and to be heroes and heroines. If reaching such high goals means delaying sex until marriage, then they'll wait. Young people are willing to sacrifice to get the best.

How little our culture understands or emphasizes sacrifice! One missionary group caught on to that truth with advertising campaigns that spell out the hard life and possible death of a

Bible translator who risks all to bring the world the gospel. I hear their most successful ad was a picture of a strong, athletic-looking man wading across a jungle river, pants rolled up, shirt unbuttoned (to expose a muscular chest, of course), a canteen hanging from his hip, and an Indiana Jones-style hat on his head. The caption reads, "Jim was voted 'most likely to succeed.' Now look at him. It's too bad. Jim had it made. Personality, initiative, a college degree with honors. Success and the 'good life' were his for the asking.

"Now look at him. Backpacking across some jungle river. Giving his life to a preliterate people barely out of the Stone Age. Painstakingly creating a written alphabet from a pre-viously unrecorded babble of sounds. Working day and night translating the pages of the New Testament. Exposing the senselessness of superstition and ignorance. Relieving pain and introducing the possibility of good health. Building a bridge of love and understanding to a neglected people. And to think . . . Jim could've been a success." Then the clincher: "If you think you're interested in Jim's kind of success . . ."

Makes you want to sign up right now. The drawing card is the offer to be a hero. People are looking for something big enough to die for. Not finding that, they'll settle for comfort and pleasure. Sociologist Tony Campolo put things in the right perspective when he once said, "Youth was made for heroism and not for pleasure." He added, "Young people are lost not because the gospel is too hard, but because it is made too easy."

There is a built-in instinct for self-sacrifice among teenagers. They seem to have no qualms about taking on the hardest challenges possible which is why former Assembly of God pastor Loren Cunningham struck a gold mine when he founded Youth With A Mission in 1960. It has become an effective missionary group partly because it put young people on the field with about five months training instead of nipping their enthusiasm in the bud by making them wade through a year or two of seminary or Bible school. That was the practice of mission boards at the time. Teenagers' zeal, enthusiasm, energy, and capacity to go without much sleep are at their maximum during those years. My own decision to accept Christ came at this strategic time of life, a little more than a month after I turned sixteen.

Although I wasn't all that savvy about life then, I knew enough to perceive that a commitment to Christ meant postponing sex until marriage. The decision I made then to stay a virgin kept me on course throughout high school, college, and in the difficult years after college while beginning a career. What helped me to forego sexual involvement was keeping very busy. During my high school years in Redmond, Washington I was active in Young Life, which wasn't the in thing to join that it later became. So we Young Lifers were looked down on a lot as "Jesus freaks," which toughened me toward teasing and prepared me for criticism in college. I worked long hours on the school yearbook and newspaper. I babysat, worked summer jobs, and wrote high school girls' sports for a weekly paper. During my senior year, I organized the school's first road rally and got involved in student government. I was a letter woman for the girls' gymnastics team, which meant practices after school for five months of the year. Any budding sexual energy that didn't get used up there got satisfied by regular Saturday ski outings in the Cascade Mountains and long-distance (two hundred miles or more) bike trips around Puget Sound in the summers.

No wonder I had little time or inclination to date during high school and looking back, I'm glad I didn't. I rarely dated. Dates only took me away from all my activities. Life was full enough without dating or sex. Besides, all the good-looking and spiritual Christian men in the area were either in Young Life or they came Saturday nights to a prayer meeting known around the Seattle area as simply "Lewises," after the couple who hosted it. Tons of people came through that log cabin in Redmond during the early 1970s and the spiritual goings-on there were heady and exciting. A date would've been boring compared to the great times we all had.

I never thought I'd be so cautious about dating, but I think the methods by which our society allows teenagers to go out unescorted is an open invitation to sex. Americans may close their eyes to this, but some cultures see this quite plainly. Houston has a Muslim population of about forty thousand, some of whom I've interviewed. Their families are quite adamant about their daughters' behavior and basically these girls spend no time alone with a man until they marry him. And they think that Americans are very loose and immoral, which is doubly indicting when added to their perceptions of America as a Christian nation. My Muslim interviewees point out that teenage pregnancy, drugs, and crime are unknown among them. A 1986 Harris poll released by Planned Parenthood showed that 57 percent of America's seventeen-year-olds, boys and girls, have had sex. Early dating contributed to this, according to a *USA Today* poll that described findings published by Brigham Young University on dating. Basically, these findings said that the earlier teenagers date, the earlier they have sex. Their survey of twenty-four hundred teenagers showed that 91 percent of the girls who began dating at twelve lost their virginity by high school graduation compared to the 56 percent who dated at thirteen, 53 percent who dated at fourteen, 40 percent who dated at fifteen and 20 percent who dated at sixteen. These people become part of the two million unmarried couples—an all-time high—that the Census Bureau estimates cohabit in America.

We certainly have our challenges laid out before us. *Time* magazine has stated that at current rates, 40 percent of today's fourteen-year-old girls will be pregnant at least once by the age of twenty. A few Christians have risen to the challenge of combatting this. Colleen Mast, a housewife and educator from Illinois, used the "challenge and save 'em" approach when she organized a group of teenagers to tell others about the virtues and rewards of chastity and abstinence. She founded MASH (McNamara Ambassadors of Sexual Health) at McNamara High School, a Catholic parochial school in Kankakee, Illinois. The program spread to parochial schools in several states and Mast got a $300,000 federal grant to develop and test a pro-chastity program in public schools called "Sex Respect." Josh McDowell's Dallas ministry sponsored a "Why Wait" essay contest in which youth write about the virtues of sexual abstinence. At least in some places, people are realizing that the church has the only sexual code that makes sense and the best contraceptive is the word "no."

These efforts definitely deserve applause. Remember, although teenagers have gotten the lion's share of publicity regarding decisions on sex, there's just as heavy a battle being fought by people in their twenties who are also being tempted to resort to sex outside of marriage. This is the great neglected age group in church ministries where people just out of college are extremely vulnerable to depression and anxiety. They may have resisted sexual temptations throughout college, only to give in during their first year out. Again, the principle of challenge and sacrifice apply to these young career people. My church in Lake Oswego, Oregon, near Portland, offered just the right thing for people my age: a system of discipleship whereby you move into a household, pool your salary, share your car, learn to serve and lay your life down for others, and grow in knowledge of God. It was a very strict lifestyle and household residents weren't allowed to date. The theory was that you were to concentrate on strengthening your relationship to Christ instead of being distracted by the opposite sex. People in their twenties flocked there in droves because the worship and lifestyle we experienced were at the cutting edge of church life. Household members moved into church leadership. At one point I think we had nearly eighty people living in the community system, including seventeen people in one household. It was one great adventure to us and we were deeply challenged.

Compare that to the "if you can't beat 'em, join 'em" approach used by other Christian groups. This is based on the premise that America is so post-Christian in its sexual morality that we should applaud any commitment we can find, rather than impose high Christian standards on a people who wouldn't abide by them anyway. The Episcopal Diocese of Newark, New Jersey, obligingly provided an example of this in January 1987 when a diocesan task force released a controversial statement suggesting that the diocese take a year to mull over whether it should bless sexual relationships between the unmarried, the widowed, the divorced, young adults, and homosexuals. Quite an uproar ensued and more than three dozen bishops from Southern United States dioceses signed a counter document that insisted the church should only bless sexual relationships within marriage. So many Episcopal bishops wrote Presiding Bishop Edmond Browning of their concerns that Browning had to draft a special letter to them three months later. In January 1988, the Newark diocese passed a resolution making final their 1987 proposal to bless sex outside of marriage.

I called the bishop of Newark, John Spong, to ask how he, the father of three grown daughters, could support the task force.

"Recalling people to a standard that has been abandoned won't work," he told me. "If they won't abstain, how do you get them to make responsible sexual decisions instead of irresponsible decisions? We need to enter into the arena and dialogue where the real values are. I don't think that virginity is a value that ought to be preserved if it creates other difficulties." He suggested that traditional moral standards were out of touch with current realities.

I certainly agree that Christians need to penetrate the real world more to realize the sexual basis on which much of our society bases its enjoyment of life. But we can't abandon our standards to do so. Old Testament prophets like Jonah and Jeremiah certainly faced a society that had abandoned all they stood for, yet they continued to preach to them. One of Spong's opponents was a Wisconsin bishop, William Wantland, a former trial lawyer who said his experience with domestic cases showed him that sex outside of marriage was anything but ideal.

"In my years of experience as a trial lawyer, I never saw any great good come of sexual relations outside of marriage," he said during a debate with Spong. "The pain and suffering caused by these relations greatly outweighed any joy or happiness. Homosexual unions were anything but gay, a misnomer if I ever saw one."

Lutherans have also agonized over the issue. A study done by the American Lutheran Church before the ALC merged with two other Lutheran bodies asked whether marriage had any meaning if a couple consummated their relationship before reaching the altar. The order of things had already been reversed since the tie was being sealed before it was made. Like the Newark document, the ALC study called upon Lutherans to decide whether traditional Christian morality had gone by the wayside in the face of widespread disregard for it.

Church laity have mirrored their leaders' confusion. A 1986 Gallup religion poll reported that among the major denominations that teach that premarital sex is immoral, only the Southern Baptists tend to agree with their leaders. A majority of Catholics and mainline Protestants believe that premarital sex is acceptable, the pool said.

There are signs that Catholic bishops are laying down the line when it comes to blessing marriages of couples who live together. In October, 1987, the Diocese of Galveston-Houston gained national publicity when it announced that cohabitating couples would not get the benefit of a large and lavish church wedding unless they moved apart for six months before marriage. Those who insisted on continuing to live together during marriage preparation would only get a small and simple ceremony, much like a "covalidation" or church blessing, of a civil ceremony. The Diocese of St. Cloud, Minnesota had gone further in 1984 by refusing to marry all couples who were living together unless they moved apart before marriage. Only for "compelling pastoral reasons" can a priest of that diocese break that rule.

Jews vary widely in their opinions on the subject, yet I found an interesting statement about sex in *The Second Jewish Catalogue,* compiled by Sharon and Michael Strassfeld.

"Contemporary Americans tend to regard sex as a biological necessity and to condone casual sex among consenting adults," they wrote. "In a sense, this attitude is an extension of the 'It's-OK-as-long-as-I-don't-hurt-anybody' mentality that is rampant today. Jewishly, this attitude has absolutely no validity. Every act has significance, because in Judaism people are not ultimately responsible solely to themselves or even to one another. We bind ourselves to a higher law and try, insofar as we are able, to conduct our lives within these boundaries." Elsewhere they added, "Marriage thus prevents the ultimate human relationship from being trivialized; it does the same for sex itself. Being the most ultimate, the sexual is reserved for the most total of relationships."

That "higher law" for Christians and Jews is God's Word. ABC TV *Nightline* host Ted Koppel has said that what Moses brought down from Mount Sinai was not the Ten Suggestions. Our society has lost a sense of shared values, especially in the realm of sexual conduct. Richard Neuhaus foresaw this in his book *The Naked Public Square* which presents a case for certain shared values that would become a public ethic. American society is pluralistic enough that in its artistic expressions, such as movies and plays, the most extreme view is presented. Certain moral points of reference, such as chastity, are tossed aside. Neuhaus warns of a moral pluralism that will result when Americans can no longer agree on even these moral points of reference. When this happens, anarchy results.

What is sad is when many in the church follow suit. There must be more support for chastity from Christians. This won't happen until they acknowledge Scripture as the moral point of reference on sexual matters. And Scripture points to chastity as a requirement to pleasing God, never as an option.

THREE

Waiting for God's Best

WAITING IS ONE OF THOSE CHRISTIAN virtues that is talked up a lot but rarely practiced. We are more accustomed to microwave Christianity. That is why I didn't expect a lecture on waiting the summer I attended a singles conference at a large Southern Baptist church in Ft. Lauderdale.

The first day of the conference was a typically sizzling hot July morning, even for South Florida, and a group of us were huddled in an air-conditioned classroom, awaiting Jackie Kendall, a speaker from West Palm Beach. Finally, in came Jackie to tell us about "Waiting for God's Best," her lecture based on the Book of Ruth. Her thesis was that those, like Ruth, who persist in virtue despite seemingly hopeless circumstances, end up getting the right mates whereas people who jump the gun and compromise their moral stands will end up disappointed. Ruth, she said, was faithful to her mother-in-law even though seemingly she was giving up her chance for a husband in doing so. She ended up marrying Boaz, a forerunner of Christ. She waited for God to bring this about, however. Modern-day women often are not content to wait and instead try to force circumstances to provide them a husband before the time is ripe, said Jackie, adding that some women do this by assenting to sex before marriage.

"When you surrender to pre-marital sex, you get post-marital insecurity," she said. "Sexual purity before marriage is a security. Fornication sets you up for adultery."

Jackie amused us all by relating how she waited until her mid-twenties to marry by holding out for a man who believed in sexual purity. She got the husband she wanted. Paraphrasing Isaiah 64:4, she said, "God works on behalf of her who waits." Then she added a note on sex before marriage: "If you maneuver to get," she said, "you maneuver to keep." It's curious how a *Time* magazine I found printed in 1973 at the height of the sexual revolution bore out her theory. Its July 9 issue reported that even back then, young people wanted less freedom rather than more freedom in terms of sexual restraint. Instead of being universally liberating, the new morality was causing insecurity, the article said, now that people couldn't even depend on marriage as a means to keep one's partner.

It is hard to wait for that which we so desperately want. Milton wrote a sonnet on the feelings of uselessness that are so common when we are forced to be still, based on the helplessness he felt as a blind man. He ended with the famous line, "They serve who also stand and wait." "They who wait on the Lord renew their strength", says Isaiah 40:31. Waiting implies trust in God, and when our trust in God is low, we don't want to wait. But if we bolt and try to find a wife or husband on our own, the rewards can be bitter. "Unless the LORD builds the house," Psalm 127:1 says, "its builders labor in vain."

I've had friends who wouldn't wait. One, whom I'll call Gwen, has a child by a man she was sleeping with. She eventually left him, but her sexual experience had so marked her that she no longer had the perception needed for choosing a husband. Sexual pleasure had distorted that perception and guilt interfered with her good judgment. So she went from one bed to another. She recently turned down a very decent job offer to follow her current lover to another city, but like all the others, she has not been able to get a commitment from that man to marry her. Gwen happens to have a relationship with the Lord but her relationships with men are far stronger. Once she's had sex with them, try as she might, she can't let them go. She is an emotional prisoner.

In contrast, the courting and marriage of two celibates results in sexual harmony because they have learned to control their passions. Contemporary psychology assumes that sexual abstinence is impossible: that we need frequent sex in the same way we need three meals a day. Unlike food, sex can be subjected to a long-term, even permanent fast. If we break the fast before the divinely ordained time, we spoil the meal. Abstinence from sex, like abstinence from sugar, results in an ability to do without it altogether. Abstinence becomes habit. Just as our bodies have to be trained to get into the habit of sex—ask any virginal newlyweds if this isn't true—so they can be trained to do without it. I think we are afraid to find this out about ourselves because we fear that if we learn how to stay sexually pure, we will be permanently inhibited. No, delayed gratification is a valuable tool in dealing with life and it works in sexual matters. It produces purity and no bad memories. It gives us the freedom to have deep friendships with the understanding they won't result in sex. The roles are clearly established; we know our boundaries with each other. We learn each other's subtleties without the hazing of sexual excitement. We value ourselves more when we know we're waiting for God's best, whether a mate or God himself, without auctioning ourselves off to the highest bidder.

What's so sad is that many people don't even wait for the highest bidder. They settle for the first offer. One celibate male friend put it more bluntly by saying, "If you've ever observed people who live promiscuously, you've noticed their personalities wane shallow. They tend to see much of life in terms of the least common denominator, namely, having sex. Staying celibate has been invaluable for personality development and just being human."

One way I've found to bloom instead of wilt on the vine is by looking for romance—not the courtship kind but the destiny kind. This kind of romance is the expectation, anticipation, joy, hope, and desire we experience as we lay down our lives for other people. Romance is what we get when we give our lives away. It happens when we face death. Jim Elliot, the famous missionary to Ecuador who was killed by the Auca Indians in 1956, wrote, "He is no fool who gives what he cannot keep to gain what he cannot lose." That kind of sentiment comforts me to know I'm not an utter fool when I spend time doing something for someone else, when I take hours that most singles would use barhopping or on dates to go to a church function. Or volunteer my time to do something I hope will pan out towards building the kingdom of God. When we die to ourselves and put the pleasures of the single life last, we really grow up and get a clearer picture of what life is all about.

In *Through the Looking Glass,* Lewis Carroll illustrated the principle of reaching our goals by surrendering our rights to them. He shows Alice heading towards a hill in the middle of a garden, but every time she heads straight for the hill, she ends up further away. She is finally advised to walk away from the hill and to her surprise, she soon ends up at the base of it. The pain and dying to ourselves in small, everyday sacrifices clears our vision for what is truly precious in life. We are working for higher ends than just our own, for greater causes than how many sexual experiences we can have.

Romance comes into our life with Christ. The decision to choose Christ instead of ourselves is a sort of "road less traveled by" that the earlier made, the better. Anyone who decides to keep their virginity past the age of fifteen comes to that spiritual wrestling match sooner or later. With me, it was a series of decisions. I read a book on how well God knows our hearts. I gathered that if we don't wish our hearts to be broken by various love affairs, we should turn them over to God, who would safeguard us from romantic heartbreak. I did this. I prayed that God would "take" my heart so that he would choose who I'd fall in love with and when. Back then, I had no idea it would be so long a wait, but I must say that my simple gesture of giving him full rights to my heart has steered me clear of a lot of shipwrecks. Some people have told me that perhaps my decision has kept me too inviolate—that I've been prevented from finding the right man as well as the wrong one. To think that way slanders God. It presupposes that he doesn't know what he is doing.

The Bible says that God searches our hearts. I believe that he, like a good Jewish father, is on the lookout for good matches for his children. Waiting on God puts the burden on him to bring this miracle to pass. Like the servant Abraham sent hundreds of miles to Haran from Beersheba in search of a bride for his son, Isaac, God is just as concerned about the right marriages for his children. That story in Genesis always encourages me, for a few hundred miles to them is like thousands of miles to us. God went to great lengths to put that unlikely match together.

Of course, God may not bring us a mate. This is an increasing possibility that chills the hearts of many single people in the frantic free sexual market that is today's American society. Many people simply aren't marrying. So we have this tension of whether to put our lives and careers on hold while we look or go full-steam ahead with our lives, letting the chips fall where they may. I am an advocate of the second option. I spent my first eight years out of college in Oregon, Florida, and now Texas. Singleness has helped me risk, grow, and live in ways that wouldn't be possible were I married. But I have friends who refused to leave a particular city for fear that they'd erase their chance of marriage. So they sit and stagnate. Remember, God does call some of us to remain single, even if the opportunity to marry presents itself. The Apostle Paul chose to be single, in a society where men were expected to marry, so he could carry out the opportunity of a millenium: preaching the gospel to all the known world.

While we wait for whatever or whomever God will bring us, we could follow the advice of Richard Foster, a theology professor and writer-in-residence at Friends University in

Wichita, Kansas. Foster suggests making a vow of fidelity that promises faithfulness to God's call for chastity in and out of marriage. The Song of Solomon, he says, has a lot to say about sexual restraint, although we traditionally view it as a description of sexual passion. Song of Solomon 3:5 and 8:4, asks that the "daughters of Jerusalem . . . do not rouse or awaken love until it so desires." This is sage advice for those of us who feel frantic about not being married, for love cannot be manipulated. In chapter eight, Foster says that the brothers who describe their sister as a wall or a door are actually saying that if she kept herself a wall, this means she kept her passions in check, reserving herself for her permanent lover. As a door, she would be opening herself to temporary liaisons. In verse ten of the same chapter, the woman proudly announces, "I am a wall, and my breasts are like towers." She did not give in to lust. According to chapter six, the man kept himself inviolate from the "sixty queens, . . . eighty concubines, . . . and virgins beyond number" for her alone, Foster said.

Even though much has been said about God not judging sexual sin any differently than he judges non-sexual sins, Paul in 1 Corinthians 6:12-20 draws a distinction between the two. Sexual sin may not be worse than other sins, but is different, as he points out in verse eighteen, saying that sexual sin is sin against our bodies. He makes it plain that the body is not designed for fornication. When we come to know Christ personally, we drag him along as an unwilling participant when we have sexual encounters outside of marriage because our bodies are now temples of the Holy Spirit. Small wonder the Holy Spirit is so grieved. Sex belongs in a special manner to God because it makes us one flesh with our partner. Unlike other bodily appetites such as sleeping and eating, he has reserved sex for the special sphere of marriage.

Curiously enough, my promiscuous reporter friend who teased me so badly was the one who dampened forever any thought I may have had on sleeping around before marriage. Months after he moved away to work on another newspaper, he called to ask about a female colleague we both knew. Then, "Wouldn't you know," he said, laughing, "I've even slept with her and I can't remember her name."

I've heard of cavalier attitudes before, but this guy's nonchalance floored me. I had naively supposed that sleeping with a person imprinted them on your mind forever. Apparently not, in some cases. That incident taught me the uselessness of giving my heart, soul, and body to a man not my husband, only to have him forget my name a year later.

However, more people say no to sex before marriage than we think. In fact, an age of sexual conservatism may be dawning. A few years ago, a song promoting chastity, "When We're Together," topped Mexican song charts for three months. The Yale (School of Medicine) Sex Counseling Service released a report that said by the mid-1980s, students weren't panicking so much at still being virgins by graduation time. In other words, said a newspaper headline on the report, virgins are now "OK."

Religious convictions played a part in the dialogue on virgins that took place during a Phil Donahue show that first aired in the spring of 1986. On stage with the controversial talk show host were six virgins: a female legal assistant, twenty-five; a male medical student who was an Orthodox Jew, twenty-one; a female nutritionist of indeterminate age; a male Catholic nurse, twenty-three; a female college student, twenty; and a Pentecostal male college student, twenty-one. Also on the set was a sociology professor, Robert Sherwin from Miami University in Oxford, Ohio, who gave out statistics on how long people were keeping their virginity. In 1963, 40 percent of all men were virgins before they married, he said. In 1984, male virgins had fallen to 28 percent. As for women, 75 percent of those polled in 1963 were still virgins. That number tumbled to 38 percent in 1978 but then women started holding out. More women are saying no, he reported, as the percentage was now up to 43 percent by 1984.

"When man and woman create," said the Jewish medical

student, "God's a third partner. If God is involved ... evidently ... there has to be something holy about it [sex], something special about it. Why should we look at sex as being so light and casual?"

One member of the audience pointed out the fallacy in the logic that couples must sleep together before marriage to discover whether they are "sexually compatible," a catchword of the sexual revolution.

"If they have the right interests in common and they are mentally compatible, then the sex will come," the person said. Still others blamed the failures of previous marriages because of bad sex, only to be shot down by still others in the audience who argued that sexual failure alone could not ruin a marriage.

"People have said that you should be experienced before you get married and my husband and I were both virgins when we got married," one woman said. "I just felt that our first experience may have been awkward, but we loved each other and we're married nine years and have a great sexual relationship. And having experience before does not make your marriage or your relationship any different."

Another person said that infidelity before marriage tends to carry over into infidelity after marriage, the exact point that Jackie Kendall made in her speech at the Ft. Lauderdale singles conference. The most poignant remark during the Donahue show came at the end from a woman in the audience who had lost her virginity at the age of seventeen, got pregnant, then had an abortion.

"Once you've said yes, it is so hard to say no again," she said. "I had wanted to be a virgin until I was married and there's no hope for me now."

There are some practical ways to say no. One obvious way is to avoid sexually informative reading material, otherwise known as the "set your minds on things above" principle. Many women's magazines fall into this category along with the "how to" columns in bridal magazines, much of what is on the current best-seller list, the majority of novels out today, and of course any pornography. It is difficult to read such descriptive passages without doing battle with a week's worth of fantasizing. We kid ourselves that we need to bone up on technique for research purposes. MTV is fascinating but a definite turn-on. Obviously I believe in being informed as a Christian of what's going on in the world. But in being open-minded, I think we must be wise. Reading sexually stimulating material while trying to remain celibate is like reading *Gourmet* magazine while sticking to a diet. We only have so much resistance and once our minds are won over to a concept, it is not long before our bodies follow. We must not assume that purity means naiveté. It certainly hasn't worked that way with me; my first job as a police reporter required me to read the rape reports.

In conversations with sexually active friends, it is amazing how many people admit how they would choose differently were they to live their teens and twenties over. They tell me they would have stayed out of bed. Some people I know are still recovering from past sexual relationships and the rejection they experienced after a parting.

Staying chaste has protected me from rejection. Most of us have experienced other kinds of rejection throughout our lives not to need the added burden of sexual wounds. One of my divorced friends tells me again and again how she envies me my lack of sexual scars. I look at friends who are recovering from casual sexual involvements like so many beached whales and realize that whatever physical pleasure I may be missing out on cannot compensate for the emptiness that comes afterwards when a lover leaves.

"It makes sense then," writes Christian author and psychiatry professor John White, "that sexual relations be confined to marriage. For acceptance and mutual disclosure are not the activities of a moment but the delicate fabric of a lifetime's weaving. To assure their development, they need the sturdy framework of sworn commitment buttressed by social laws.... A marriage commitment is assurance against rejection and so allows for full self-disclosure by both partners."

Sex without a marriage commitment can bring disaster. One overlooked reason for teenage suicides these days is simply pain. When a teenager breaks up with someone he or she was sexually involved with, it is like a divorce. Divorce is hard enough for adults; for kids, it is devastating. Likewise, sexual split-ups are too painful for some to handle.

Many such people are ignorant of the emotional effects of sexual intercourse. As with my friend Gwen, sexual acts become unbreakable sexual bonds. The person may be desirable for the moment, but not for life. Sometimes the man or woman may end up marrying this partner out of feelings of guilt, hardly a good basis for lifelong commitment. Or they go their separate ways feeling a great loss.

"I believe," a reporter once wrote me, "that God intended sex to be a bonding experience as powerful as the bonding that takes place between a mother and a child at birth. If you constantly tear away at that bond, pretty soon you lose your ability to bond. No wonder we have so many divorces."

The emotional costs of trivializing life's most intimate relationship—except our relationship with God—is heavier than most people care to admit. In sex, we give ourselves completely to the other person. We are totally vulnerable, open, and unashamed. The couple is emotionally as well as physically naked. They have the ability to destroy each other as well as to become one flesh. That is why divorce is so devastating. The couple who was once bonded is now sundered and neither of them is quite the same. A dimension of their personalities has been amputated.

The greatest intimacy in life is sexual intercourse and the greatest commitment is marriage. Ideally, they take place on the same day. Sex is an outward act that seals and signifies the inward commitment. The continuing practice of sex within marriage reaffirms that pledge. But all that is changing. Even virginity has become a variable concept for those who adopt the "anything but" rule on acceptable sexual practices. Some say that short of full penetration, virginity can still be kept, allowing themselves extensive foreplay and a number of sexual variants. Which is why one reporter challenged me to define technical virginity for him, that is: how far is too far. I wish he could have listened in on a conversation I had with a girlfriend who described why she and her boyfriend called a halt to French kissing. Their intense kissing sent signals through both of their bodies to prepare for sex. Being Christians, they did not follow through, but the frustration of starting something they didn't wish to finish made them decide not to start it at all. In Matthew 5:28 Jesus says that lust is as bad as adultery; therefore, I think he would take a hard line on technical virginity. In this passage, he broadens the definition of chastity to avoiding even a merely lustful look. John White says there is no difference in God's eyes between petting and sex. Therefore, we should do neither. The 1 Corinthians 6:18 passage says to flee immorality, not to rate it on a scale of one to ten.

I am convinced that God cares for us. I know that as we hold out for God's best, he rewards us. My convictions date back to a haunting story, *The Three Weavers,* that I read during my childhood in a series of books known as *The Little Colonel* series, published near the turn of the century. Briefly told, the story is a fairy tale about three men who are weavers. Each had a daughter born the same day with (admittedly old-fashioned) names like Huberta, Hertha, and Hildegarde. Each girl was fated at birth to wed a prince if each fulfilled one condition: they had to weave a mantle on a loom for their prince. The mantle would have to fit him perfectly. Many other men would drop by beforehand to claim the mantle for their own. And they had a limited supply of gold thread with which to weave a mantle for a prince with none to spare for other men.

As the years unfolded, the girls chose separate ways to fulfill their goals. Hertha, whose father refused to tell her about the mantle, stumbled upon her loom one day. Fearing her father's anger, she wove her mantle in secret, but gave it to an unworthy man. When her prince came, she had nothing to give him, so her heart broke. Huberta, whose father was much more carefree and careless about his daughter's upbringing, wove various mantles and distributed them to all sorts of men. When her prince finally rode up, she had squandered too much thread and could only produce a pygmy-sized mantle. Her heart broke, too, because her prince would not accept it. But Hildegarde held out, not giving her mantle away to various suitors, reluctantly following the advice of her wise father to wait through the years. When her prince came, she had a perfect mantle waiting for him and with her father's blessing, they lived happily ever after.

Many analogies in this 1904 book are applicable to us three generations later. I often reread it to remind myself that there is reason to wait on the Lord, who, like Hildegarde's father, is willing to guide us if we only listen to him. His Spirit can cut through our perceptions that can be blinded by emotion to reveal the depths of a would-be mate. Like the gold thread, sexual purity is easily squandered and never regained. Whatever God has in store for us is worth the wait.

FOUR

One Is the Loneliest Number

I WAS AT MY COUSIN'S WEDDING. The country club dining room was filled with flowers, waiters dashing to and fro, and a band serenading the well-dressed guests. The dinner had been sublime and now the waiters were pouring the coffee as I watched my aunts, uncles, and cousins glide around the dance floor. They swished, they waltzed, they pirouetted and glided about in each other's arms. My table was all couples but me, so when the music started, I was left sitting there with the dessert plates and coffee cups.

I, who grew up taking ballet lessons and to whom dance is as natural as air, only danced once that evening and that one time was thanks to a kind uncle. I felt I could've outdanced any woman there but I was kept still for lack of a partner. And I didn't want to ask anyone. There's a place to be assertive, I felt, but the dance floor was not it. Several years ago, I would've blamed myself for the situation; this time I decided to flee to the terrace overlooking a golf course where I could watch the sunset and get some comfort from somewhere. "Well," I told the Lord, "I am lonely and what are you going to do about it?"

No divine response was forthcoming, so I returned to the reception only to learn that I had missed the tossing of the bride's bouquet. I took a "this too shall pass" stance and pulled up a chair to a table full of people. How well I know loneliness. It has been my biggest struggle in life. I think that's why over the past decade I've put so much effort into learning to hear the voice of the Lord; just a simple phrase from him eases my loneliness and keeps me going for weeks.

"The single person facing life alone may feel intimidated in the world of couples," writes Brother Benedict Groeschel in his book, *The Courage to Be Chaste.* "There is often no one waiting at the airport, no one with whom to discuss problems, no one to call when you backed your car into a tree. The minor emergencies of life frequently emphasize the single person's vulnerability and lack of support."

It's not only the emergencies that are upsetting; it's the little things like wanting to go out to lunch but finding no one at the office who cares to go along or wanting to see a movie without having to sit alone. In times like these we feel like an incarnation of Three Dog Night's famous song, "One is the Loneliest Number." Sometimes I think that loneliness is the cruelest result of the Fall.

I can remember one period of my life when I was never lonely: the two years during my mid-twenties when I lived in that Christian household system in Portland. This was during the late 1970s when Christian household-style communities were quite the vogue around the country and, wanting to be on the cutting edge, I moved into one affiliated with my church. The community had several married couples with mostly single adults in their twenties and thirties. We lived a lifestyle into which loneliness never crept. Except for our jobs, we did everything together: outings, worship, and meals. One of the women was quadriplegic and we'd simply bundle her into the front seat, put her wheelchair into the trunk, and take her along wherever we went. Our worship was rich because we spent so much time together. We felt free to confess our sins to each other which resulted in openness and unconditional acceptance. This brought about greater intimacy with each other. Thus, we felt free to risk in worship. And because of our geographical proximity, there was always someone around to do something with. Some of our greatest conversations took place over the dishes. I belonged so thoroughly to this group of people that the desire for sex rarely came to mind. There really is something to the theory that if our other needs for love and belonging are met, sex is not such a driving desire.

Richard Rohr, a Franciscan priest who founded a similar community called the New Jerusalem Community in Cincinnati in the early 1970s, once gave a series of talks on the natural family and the spiritual family. He said we all must have a spiritual family—our brothers and sisters in Christ—as well as our biological or natural families. He remarked in one talk that women are not simply longing for men; they're longing for wholeness. Men aren't simply desiring women; they too long for wholeness. He observed that people want friendship more than sex, that the school for friendship is the church and that the excessive perceived need for sex in our society can be diffused in the Christian community.

"We are all sexual," Rohr said. "Sexuality merely means the attraction of opposites.... Why is the sexual desire so strong? I think because he [God] is teaching us . . . that we're not whole and that we've got to be in relationship."

Single adults are more intimacy-starved than sexually deprived, writes counselor Harold Ivan Smith, director of Tear Catchers, a Kansas City, Missouri ministry. In his book, *Single and Feeling Good,* he defines intimacy as a feeling or emotion based on commitment. It is also having a high trust level so that we can speak the truth to others. It is having a common history, experiences, and memories. That is why moving to a new city is so hard, because we leave behind people with common experiences that we share. In the new locale, it takes about a year to get to any meaningful trust level with people. So, that intervening year is lonely.

When I first moved to Houston, that loneliness was buffered somewhat when I found a Christian roommate within 24 hours. I was also staying with a couple I had known from college and joined a church where I was able to build several close relationships in the space of a few months. Yet, I still had to hold back a little, not wishing to place too much weight on these friendships too fast. This was a difficult balancing act to maintain as I was also learning the ropes of a high-powered job where one just barges in and gets to know sources and interviewees fast. It takes time to earn a right to be heard in the lives of most people. Intimacy is a precious thing. It requires time and risk and respect for the other's dignity.

A few months after I moved to Houston, a woman in church whom I knew in a general fashion and liked a lot approached me and said, "I really like you and I want to tell you I am available to you for anything you need and if you need a friend, I want to be a friend." That really touched me. She was taking a huge risk that I wouldn't brush her off. I didn't. We began to pray together weekly and have become good friends.

However, we have to choose our close friends carefully. Certain people will never commit themselves to us. This came home to me one day when I was wandering around the site of the Houston International Festival, a week-long downtown street fair in the spring. There were colorful banners, music stands and hot dog carts. People were seated on park benches near red, pink, violet, and lavender azalea bushes with tall, ultra-modern glass-walled skyscrapers as a backdrop. Despite the impressive skyline and festive surroundings, I was lonely. I was very conscious of how almost everyone there had someone to sit and chat with, to eat alongside, or just be with, except me. Finally, I headed back toward the office and dropped by a take-out French cafe for a lunch-to-go because I didn't want to sit inside there alone. (Singles use all sorts of techniques to avoid the table set for one: room service while on business trips or meals eaten behind a steering wheel.) Then I spotted one of the reporters in my department.

"Well, hello," she said. "Are you staying here or leaving?"

"I've got to get back to work," I replied. "All I need are two croissantwiches and something to drink."

"Let's walk back together," she said. My loneliness lifted. At least someone wanted to be with me. I dashed from one cash register to another, picking up parts of my lunch, only to turn around and see the reporter disappear out the door. I couldn't imagine why she had abandoned me. I had kept her waiting not more than a minute. Then the cup of tea I was carrying started to leak and by the time I remedied that and reached the sidewalk, my erstwhile friend was out of earshot. Not once did she look back. Feeling rejection on top of loneliness, I meandered back to my office and ate lunch at my desk—the mark of a lonely person as well as a workaholic. I think some people become workaholics because they don't wish to face the fact that one is the loneliest number. We blame ourselves a lot for being lonely or we at least take it out on ourselves, making ourselves work harder or overeat. Or we hide from it all by turning up the radio, TV, and stereo. Or we resort to sex, hoping maybe that will nip loneliness in the bud.

I've heard more than one person say they're lonely because they're not having sex. And that the lack of sex makes them into cold fish. Sometimes we do this without thinking, like the people I met at a conference on celibacy at a convent in West Palm Beach, Florida. I was the only person there who was not a priest or nun. The nuns—only one priest dared come and he was the workshop leader—were astonished that I was there. They had never imagined anyone remaining celibate out of religious conviction without the binding vows of poverty, chastity, and obedience.

The priest leading the workshop and the nun assisting him asked the group to say which words first came to our minds upon hearing the word, "celibacy." True to form, we came up with negative phrases: "no sex," "aloofness," "no joy," "barrier," "cold person," "non-involvement," "deprivation," "non-emotional," "sacrifice," and "mortification." Someone plaintively added that celibates feel as though they don't belong to anyone.

The priest observed that we all long for that sense of

belonging or being owned. Sex does have a way of bringing an immediate sense of connectedness, physically and spiritually. When people want to belong or connect at a deep level, they fall back on sex for communication. To be lying in the arms of someone we love is one of the most secure feelings on earth. There is warmth, there is love, there is self-disclosure; you know someone in the most intimate way possible. The vulnerability is so complete that the couple can break quickly through formalities to know and be known, which is the same thing singles long for. But chaste singles don't have the bonding power of genital sex. Whereas husbands and wives have the mutual security to cling to in possessing each other's bodies, singles don't have that comfort.

But, said the nun, although we think we need sex, our needs are more profound. Without sex as an outlet, we must be more creative in finding other outlets. This takes work. Sexually, two partners have given each other the power to not only invade their bodies but their entire personalities. When we abstain from sex, we must make sure that we not seal ourselves off from emotions and vulnerability that a sexually active couple gets automatically. We who abstain need to risk in other areas where the stakes are high: where our bodies may not be on the line but our egos are.

We all have a certain amount of energy to put into relationships; energy that married couples use on each other and which singles can bestow on the persons of their choice. But we must choose someone or better still, a group of someones. The decision to put ourselves into intimate non-sexual relationships is the best option for the single Christian. This is what Jesus did. To risk is to live dangerously, but it makes the ride more exciting. My best description of risk comes from an anecdote, "Who's Elwood McDugle?" from a devotional printed by the Oral Roberts Evangelistic Association.

"The story is told," the narrative reads, "of a father with two sons who was trying to encourage the boys not to be afraid of taking risks for worthwhile ventures. He said, 'Think of Christopher Columbus. He risked everything to sail to a new land because he believed the world was round. We remember his name. Think of Paul Revere. He risked his life to warn his fellow patriots and because he did, we remember him.

"'Then there are the Wright brothers. They took some risks in getting the first airplane off the ground. We still remember them today.' By this time, the father had the interest of the two boys. He said, 'And then think of Elwood McDugle.'

"'Elwood McDugle,' the oldest said. 'Who's he?'

"'Ah!' said the father. 'The reason you never heard of Elwood McDugle is because he was afraid to take risks.'"

Our commitment to a chaste, single existence is a risk, a gamble that as Christians we can be content there. "Voluntary chastity," writes Groeschel, "is not a vocation for the faint-hearted." He points out that persons who mock chastity—and there are plenty—will in the next breath express admiration for Mother Teresa, not realizing that the nature of her work obligates her to be chaste. Mother Teresa has managed to draw a large number of single, chaste women into her order, the Missionary Sisters of Charity, to spend their lives on the poor and unwanted. Describing these women in a recent documentary on her life, Mother Teresa said, "The person who Christ has chosen for himself: she knows. Maybe she doesn't know how to express it, but she knows."

This image of staking one's love on God gives the chaste person a reason for being. Many single people feel that no one has much at stake in their existence and if they died, they wouldn't be missed. One of my roommates had a boyfriend who got angry at something at church and so left the congregation. He felt unneeded and unwanted. As the weeks went by, my roommate began to notice small things, gaps that he had formerly filled in with his presence. Now various tasks went undone, simply because he was not there to do them. His absence left a hole in that church body, which now functioned with an embarrassing awkwardness. We are missed. We may not literally kill ourselves, but by withdrawing our labor from the body of Christ, we commit spiritual suicide.

In various fields involving dangerous work, such as the Foreign Service or in foreign missions, the mentality crops up that single people are somehow more expendable than married people. This is true even when it comes to working weekends and holidays. We were discussing at a local journalism seminar how single people tend to get stuck with odd shifts because their supervisors assume that they have no family to be with. Unfortunately, our culture assumes that the addition of a husband or wife somehow increases our worth. This is contrary to biblical ideals. That's why I liked a phrase printed on the back of *Struggling for Wholeness,* by Ann Kiemel Anderson and Jan Kiemel Ream. "You are significant," it reads. "Even alone."

I chanced upon an article titled "Celebacy: Love 'Wasted' on God" in the Christian magazine *New Heaven, New Earth* that quoted Nano Farabaugh, a South Bend, Indiana woman, who compared celibacy to the woman in John 12:3. That was the lady who poured out ultra-expensive perfume—kind of like pouring out a quart of Giorgio—onto Jesus' feet. Rarely have I seen anyone compare virginity or celibacy to something expensive like perfume, yet this woman wrote that our sexual purity is of higher worth to God than we imagine.

"In the ten years since I committed my life to live single for the Lord, I have realized that commitment is one of pouring out something very costly," she wrote. "In choosing to give up marriage, I chose never to belong to anyone but the Lord, never to have children or grandchildren, never to have the security of a husband's love. Having had the opportunity to marry and choosing not to, I have voluntarily poured out what I treasured, as the woman did with the perfume."

Why? Because "Christ is worthy of total self-sacrifice, is worthy of receiving such an offering," she added. Nano, however, lives in a covenant Christian community, the People of Praise, which is similar to the one I knew in Portland. She probably gets lots of support there. Most single men and women are not as fortunate, such as a Wisconsin woman who responded to the *Christianity Today* article I wrote on celibacy with a letter describing her loneliness and lack of support from her evangelical church. "All I can say is 'right on,'" she wrote, "and if you ever discover the secret to being content in this miserable state, please let me in on it. Only part of me says that because I don't want to convey the message that I'm a joyless Christian, far from it, but being a forty-nine-year-old virgin is no picnic, either."

This woman's church was no support to her. Instead, what she and many singles get in church are overt and covert signals on the desirability of marriage. The typical secular mindset works against them too, making chastity sound like a dirty word. In a typical news story on sexual issues, those who promote abstinence and resist casual sex and homosexuality are seen as rigid, cold, maneuvering, immature, and asexual. Those who make a case for sex outside of marriage are seen as open, gentle, pastoral, and caring. This sort of reaction cropped up when the Vatican issued a critical statement on homosexuality in October 1986. What I gathered from some of the essays written about that statement was that the writers of the Vatican statement were seen as dried-up, passionless people who really don't understand the gusto and joy of life.

People get that impression because, in putting the brakes on our sexual drives, we are tempted to turn off our capacity for tenderness and compassion. We do this to protect ourselves, but people observing us don't see the inner anguish; all they see is the outer resolution. Thus, those who take a moral stand on sexuality aren't seen as courageous or risk-takers. This is an astonishing reversal of roles that has happened in the latter half of this century. I compare the state of a single person to a clay pitcher. Today's pressures would make us either break in pieces or harden: I suggest we fill ourselves with God's Spirit and pour ourselves out for others.

One way I combat loneliness is to have a roommate. Now

roommates aren't everything but they're healthier to our well-being than living alone. This seems to be more socially acceptable for women than men since men sometimes get stereotyped as gay if two or more of them room together. This is a shame. A roommate is the first step to sanity. We need their sharpening effect and the good and bad that comes with roommates. We must accept the tensions as well as the benefits, even if that means debating over grocery bills and who should've unloaded the dishwasher. Singles get accused of selfishness a lot, yet it is hard not to be selfish when we live alone and get everything our way. I've also held out for committed Christian roommates. I get enough of "the world" to deal with at work without having to handle a roommate whose moral views differ from mine. I'd rather not have to meet her boyfriend first thing in the morning in the bathroom. Although there's been some cost and inconvenience involved with insisting on another Christian woman to room with, I've not regretted that decision.

Customs on roommates vary according to locale and architecture. In Oregon, many singles shared large, multiple-bedroom houses because that was the cheapest method of rent. In Florida, where such houses rarely existed, singles shared a condo. All of my roommates have been invaluable supports. To find them, I've posted notices on bulletin boards of churches and Christian bookstores. After finding four roommates in the past four years, I think I must be an expert on how to locate a Christian roommate in a large metropolitan area. None of these women attended the same church as I, so I had to go outside my usual circle of acquaintances to find them. I found a roommate within a week in Miami and if that can be done in South Florida, which must be one of the most isolating, transient parts of the country, then it can be done anywhere. My roommates always became my friends and prayer partners as well.

Such friendships help cut down on the loneliness that makes us long for sex, which will never fill the emptiness in our souls.

Loneliness drives us to make desperate choices. I was at a retreat once where one gutsy woman said that as she was approaching her thirties, she despaired of finding any man to love. Feeling that men had failed her, she turned to women and ended up in a lesbian relationship that still didn't fill the void in her life. She eventually got out of that lifestyle and found her present church where at last she found people to love and care for her.

Loneliness is a most devastating way of persuading people that chastity is not for them. It is hard for us to see the other side of the coin: promiscuity is no bed of roses, either. I was reading about ballerina Gelsey Kirkland's book, *Dancing on My Grave,* which mentions her affair with Mikhail Baryshnikov. I was struck with how empty such liaisons left her. Even with a glamorous lover like him, here was love without commitment, which really wasn't love at all. She described how, before he slept with her, she hoped that she meant something special to him. All she ended up being was another conquest. On stage, meanwhile, they were partners who needed a kind of working intimacy in order to draw out the best in each other. All she could see was his demand for intimacy without commitment. This was emptiness to her. "How," she wrote, "could I dance without love?"

It's best to look for intimacy and love from people who don't demand sex along with it. When I choose my close friends, I look for people who think like I do. Of course, I get along with people who don't, but intimacy involves a certain empathy with my basic convictions. I look for people who listen to me and seek me out as much as I seek them out. It is too easy to get attached to people who I call drainers: those who want comfort and advice but who don't take any time to draw me out. My journalistic training has so schooled me to listen and draw others out that at home and church I automatically fall into that reporter role. That can get lethal. After a while, I realize that all I have been doing is listening to people non-stop for several weeks. So I have to force myself to volunteer information about my thoughts since people rarely ask what they are.

Loneliness for me is a battle that may never stop, so I try not to get disheartened when the going gets rough. Some people glibly suggest we can choose not to be lonely. Such denial has never worked for me. I've found it more helpful to allow myself to experience, although not be overcome by, the reigning emotion of the time. If it is loneliness, then I need to walk through it. Only by experiencing the pain can I go beyond it. My loneliest times are when God's voice is faint or silent, which trebles my feelings of loneliness. At that point, feelings are all that count and no amount of cheery logic can dispel that.

Only faith brings us through such hard times. For my college yearbook, I was asked to choose a quote that summed up my life thus far. So I chose two verses in Psalm 42 that helped me during my loneliest moments in college:

> Deep calleth unto deep at the noise of thy waterspouts:
>   all thy waves and thy billows are gone over me.
> Yet the Lord will command his lovingkindness in the
>   daytime,
>   and in the night his song shall be with me,
>   and my prayer unto the God of my life. Psalm 42:7-8

FIVE

Sex and the Single Christian Woman

A S I WRITE, the purring black and white kitten in my lap is aiding my creative efforts by happily chewing on portions of the manuscript. The more vital the paragraph, the better food for his hungry little pink mouth. When we're not tussling over the pages, he is snoozing nearby, having sensed that I am by nature warm and comfortable and that I've no intentions of hurting him.

Tenderness and warmth aren't exactly the two most necessary traits I've needed during eight years of working on daily newspapers. Many women of my generation have had to develop traits our mothers never thought of, mainly because they married soon after they graduated from college. Many of my peers did not marry early, and having no husband as a support, we have had to go it on our own. To get anywhere in newspaper reporting, which is a very competitive profession, I had to have savvy and be aggressive and demanding to beat out the competing papers for stories. Especially in South Florida, where I was up against two larger dailies, the demands on me and my fellow reporters to be earlier and better on stories—with less resources than the larger papers had—turned life into a pressure cooker. In a few short years, I learned how to shove aside feelings of inferiority and take on the world. I had to in order to survive because, unlike women of an earlier generation, I had no husband to fall back on should I fail. And I dealt mostly with men who were far older than I: police officers, politicians, clergy, city and county government employees, some of whom at times lied to me or assumed that because I was female, I would be naive. This occasionally worked to my advantage: people were caught off guard because I was a woman, so by the time they woke up to my machinations, I already had the necessary facts and documentation in hand.

These same qualities didn't stand me in good stead at church, however. I'll admit that the qualities of a young career woman aren't all that compatible with traditional Christian ideas of femininity. I might add that the rules on the role of a woman in her twenties have undergone a massive shift in the past generation. These days, such a woman, single or married, is expected to work. A generation ago and all the preceding generations before that, she was not. As I've moved out of my claw-my-way-to-the-top twenties into my slightly mellower thirties, I've noticed how gentleness, empathy, and politeness softens interviewees a lot faster than hard and fast questions.

Recently, I found a list of positive female traits, most of which I consider to be realistic, compiled by philosophy professor Ronda Chervin in her recent, *Feminine, Free and Faithful*. She lists:

responsive	tender	wise
compassionate	hospitable	perceptive
empathetic	receptive	sensitive
enduring	diplomatic	spiritual
gentle	considerate	sincere
warm	polite	obedient
intuitive	supportive	trusting
vulnerable (in	graceful	sweet
the sense of	expressive	charming
being emotionally	quiet	faithful
open)	pure	sensually perceptive (vs being prudish)

This is not to say men can't show these qualities; indeed those who do in the best way are fatherly, she wrote, but these are qualities that women should especially have. Married women find these qualities naturally develop during moments of sexual surrender, pregnancy, birth, breast feeding, and mothering, she said.

I've been fortunate to have my mother as a model for many of these qualities. As a willowy blond-haired college student from Philadelphia, she was in her early twenties when she married my father, a Coast Guard officer who rose to admiral twenty-five years later. Life as a Coast Guard wife with its frequent moves kept her from holding a job, but she kept up her academic interests by getting a master's degree in zoology while we three children were in elementary school. I was picked on and teased by neighborhood kids during much of my childhood, so I'd go to my mother for solace. Thank God my mother didn't work, because when I'd come home crying, she was always there to listen. She still listens and is immensely perceptive, empathetic, supportive, intuitive, and wise. I continue to lean on her for a lot of advice.

I think the challenge to single Christian women is to develop the same qualities without the aids our mothers had. It's a difficult task, especially when there is little to encourage our femininity and much to tear it down. The worst day of the year for the single woman is Valentine's Day, when vases of flowers, balloon bouquets, and boxes of candy magically appear on the desks of the women who have thoughtful husbands or lovers. On my most recent Valentine's Day, I had scurried over to the bank two blocks away from work to cash a check just when many businesses were closing. I noticed the women pouring out of elevators and office buildings, seemingly all of them with flower bouquets and potted plants tucked under their arms. All those red and white ribbons and lace overwhelmed me, who had no flowers on my desk to cart home, no gooey candies to eat, no sentimental cards to read.

Valentine's Day is for the single woman what Mother's Day

is to the infertile married woman: a reminder of her lack. Valentines from parents and roommates just aren't sufficient. Even silly Valentines from men affirm us as desirable human beings. Remember those days in elementary school when valentines would get passed out and it was plain who was the most popular girl in the class and who was not? Things don't change all that much when we grow up. No matter how stunningly we're dressed, the lack of something as inconsequential as a valentine makes us feel we're not good enough, that we'll never make it with men. When we see a woman whom we perceive as not very physically attractive getting attention and love from her husband, we despair. We don't begrudge her the man she's found, but why not us?

The modern answer to that is that we are not looking hard enough. My mother sent me an Associated Press story on a Miami lawyer who specializes in teaching single women how to get married. The article said four hundred clients have passed her course in the past eighteen years. Her message was that in order to marry well, you must actively look for a husband and not leave love and marriage to chance. This goes directly against the grain of every Christian book for singles I've ever read. The latter types advise the woman to wait and trust God and the man to initiate. Well, plenty of single women have taken that advice—and we're still single. The despair that exists among many single Christian women could be lightened if we could grasp how to develop our female sexuality without waiting for a man to do it for us. Christian author Ann Kiemel Anderson, who got married at thirty-five, writes in *Struggling for Wholeness* how sexual overtures from single and married Christian men only frightened and repulsed her. She knew Scripture forbade her to engage in sex, yet here were all these opportunities from supposedly virtuous sources. One day she realized that her sexuality and femininity came from within and did not need to be proven. This gave her an inner security to withstand further pressures from men. It also helped her to give her life away by caring for others. The more she tended to the wounded and the broken, the less her sexual desires overwhelmed her. "Never before had i felt i had captured femininity and true sexual appeal," she wrote in her lowercase style. "Never before had i lived with such serenity and self worth."

Her sister Jan Kiemel Ream adds that our sexuality is not wrapped up in belonging to a man. But our society perceives that it is, as do many single women who think they are defective because no one has yet chosen to marry them. So they do almost anything to prove their worth as women. Ream notes that the most passionate women in the world are single women out to prove they are valuable. It's disheartening to be at a women's function at church only to hear woman after woman introduce herself as married to a certain man and the mother of x amount of children. When we introduce ourselves, we single women need something else to say. When I notice the immense varieties of activities that I and other single women engage in at work and church, I have to agree with Ream. The same principle doesn't hold true for single men, who, because they are much in demand in Christian circles, don't need to prove themselves.

There's an immense crisis of confidence among single Christian women today. We perceive what the church ignores: that baby boomer women far outnumber men. Unlike our secular counterparts, we don't have the outlet of casual sex, which most women's magazines take for granted as a part of every single woman's life. A few years ago, a *Newsweek* article created waves among our ranks when it printed an analysis of a demographic study called "Marriage Patterns in the United States." The study, which was compiled by three Yale sociologists, said that white, college-educated women born in the mid-1950s who were still single at thirty had only a 20 percent chance of marrying. By the age of thirty-five, the odds dropped to 5 percent. Women at the age of forty, with odds at 2.6 percent, were more likely to be killed by a terrorist. The odds were even worse for up-scale black women. It was the most detailed entry to date of a growing collection of articles on the plight of highly educated but single women who cannot find men. Even though the study has since been contested on the grounds that it used insufficient data, the article included some telling comments that I've often heard repeated among single female Christians. A sociologist was quoted as saying "When you look at men who don't marry, you're often looking at the bottom of the barrel. When you look at the women who don't marry, you're looking at the cream of the crop." Put this with the tendency of single women to marry up in status rather than marrying down and you've got a large group of women who will never marry.

I remember talking this over with another Christian career woman who was disconsolate over not finding stable Christian men. She was a manager moving up in her company. Tired of waiting for a mate, she was saving to buy her own home.

"It's not that there isn't anybody around," she said. "There's"—and she named a few Christian men we both knew. "But they're not going anywhere," she continued. "Here I am, making a good salary, saving my money, having a career, and setting goals in my life while most of these guys barely have jobs, much less good ones that I'd even consider letting them support me on if we'd have children and I'd have to quit work. I don't trust them. They don't seem to be going anywhere spiritually either; I am around this church a lot and I rarely see these guys volunteer or help out in anything. And they're no busier than I am. Why should I marry someone like that?"

Richard Foster in *Money, Sex and Power* points out that churches order their singles to marry only other Christians, but limit women to a field of rapidly shrinking men. If they don't care for these men, they're labeled as picky. Due to its methods of evangelism and the tenor of many church services, women are more attracted to Christianity than men. This is not the case in Islam and Orthodox Judaism, I've noticed, because those religions give men the primary place in the keeping of their commandments and religious observances. Perhaps

Christianity is more egalitarian than it gives itself credit for, but it is true that many church services will major on the gentle and sweet aspects of faith while downplaying the prophetic and challenging. Men (and some women, too) are more attracted to the latter and most men aren't going to put up with feminized church services.

Christian women perceive rightly that the good Christian men tend to get picked off (for marriage) in their early twenties. Even the casual observer can perceive that most single men, starting with teenage boys, are not in church. They're more often at the beach, at the races or on the ski slopes. So, unless we disobey God outright by marrying a non-Christian, let's face it squarely: many of us women will never marry. My generation is producing large quantities of celibate Christian women. Our best friends need to help us face up to this fact instead of spinning the fairy tale that all we need to do is believe God for a mate. He doesn't always throw in a godly husband when we accept Christ. Assuming that God will provide a husband sounds spiritual, but tell that to a virtuous forty-year-old woman whose biological clock is striking midnight. She would have done better to face the possibility of perpetual singleness ten years ago.

It's therefore a cruel irony that pressures to get married come not only from ourselves and our families but also from our churches, where never to have gotten married is never to have succeeded. Or people view us as immature because we haven't had to deal with the so-called real problems of the world like they have with kids, bills, marital battles, and so on. Or married women think we single women are aggressive and pushy, not realizing that those of us who didn't marry early on like they did have had to be aggressive to survive. We don't have husbands who can fix our cars, do our finances, or haggle with the landlord.

The single career woman is a recent innovation in Western society. In past years, she lived with her parents or brothers, a practice still followed in other cultures, where to live alone is considered an aberration. No longer are we sheltered by fathers or brothers. Instead, we are free agents living thousands of miles from our families. I think I surprised my father a few years ago when I asked him to take on the responsibility of praying every Sunday that I would find the right man to marry. Arranged marriages aren't in style these days, but I wanted to let him know I felt he still has a role to play in helping bring about my future happiness.

What we pick up on Christian womanhood often doesn't deal with present-day realities—or ignores them. Women's liberation, in its broadest sense, has incredibly altered the social landscape during our lifetimes. We compete in the job market, we network, we don't deprecate ourselves, we marry later, and we're in church leadership more. There is plenty to read on female sexuality. Abortion is legal. Daycare is a fact of life. As Christians, we may disagree or abhor what the winds of change have tossed on our society's shores, but we can't close our minds to what is already a *fait accompli*.

The secular workplace is kinder to the single woman than is the church. In our jobs, we're used to moving up and being rewarded. In church leadership, things don't quite work that way and we find we hit an unseen barrier once we pass a certain level. Single women are occasionally included in semi-leadership functions, but when it comes to really calling the shots, the task gets handed to a married woman. The unspoken assumption is that married women are safer because they have someone they must answer to whereas single women do not. Getting married is such a rite of passage in the church and most people don't know how to define those of us who are not linked up. As a religion writer, I get tons of mail from religious organizations hawking various conferences. In each slick conference brochure I handle, nearly every female speaker listed is married, which conveys the message that only married women have something to say. This is not representative of the typical church, where many of those attending have never married or are widowed or divorced.

Even at church, where the trust levels are high, single women need to guard themselves from giving off signals they don't intend. Much depends on whether the church is formal or informal, like mine where people hug each other as a sort of Christian social gesture and to express openness. I've developed my own set of rules on this. I'll hug a brother in Christ while in a group or in public view somewhere, but when I'm alone in a room with the same man, I would rather not touch him. No matter how innocent a hug can be, someone walking into that scene suddenly can make all sorts of conjectures. It's the appearance of evil that Scripture talks about that concerns me. I find that single women are automatically more suspect in being the temptress where sexual liaisons are concerned. Churches can be a minefield as well as a blessing for the single woman. Remember, it was a single woman who ended up having a sexual liaison with Jim Bakker. Her sexual performance during that encounter was as much discussed in the press as was his. The most vulnerable party is the single woman who needs to know that her reputation, as well as that of the man, must be protected.

This is true with the pastor of any church, whom a lot of single women and unhappily married women cling to because he is the one man who will listen and sympathize with them. A single woman at one church I attended practically threw herself at the pastor. He couldn't hide the trapped look on his face. With men, I wait until they initiate a hug and then I respond. I prefer to be pursued. That is one way I exercise my femininity. I find this attitude of waiting attracts rather than repels; in fact, in a typical church fellowship hall where casual hugs are accepted, men tend to express affection to single women more than married women because the former don't have a husband hovering around them. This is okay up to a point. I remember two instances just after college where I felt that men were being too intimate in the ways they touched me. Moreover, I knew their behavior would be radically different were I married. In both instances, I had to confront them and it is by the grace of God that I pulled it off by using few words and not apologizing for my feelings. In dealing with married couples, I try to become as good a friend with the wife as I am with the husband to assure her nonverbally that I have no designs on him. This has meant a lot of work on my part, especially in relationships where I am better friends with the husband, but it has paid off.

When someone has made unwelcome advances towards me at a church, I've usually avoided that man or taken a good male friend into my confidence, asking him to hover around me for a few Sundays until the first man gets the message and leaves me alone. If I'm the one being tempted sexually—which is easy in church because we are all emotionally bonded to each other—I find a friend outside of church in whom I can confide. Together, we map out a solution. Being tempted does not reflect badly on us; in fact, it is only natural that these things should happen in churches where the hottest contests on earth between God and Satan occur. It is only natural that our enemy should concentrate his forces on the Christian encampment and stir up sexual temptations. We must show the world that we can defeat this tendency to sin. As Luther once said, you cannot prevent birds from flying around your head, but you can keep them from building a nest in your hair.

However, we still must deal with our sexual energy in some fashion. Lacking the traditional outlets, I use it up through long hours at work, by jogging, or in strong church involvement. It's an exhausting lifestyle but at least I'm too tired at night to think of much else but sleep. I've also had friends in whom I could confide. What is helpful are older women who have time to listen and who won't lecture us on how our standards for a husband are too high, a common accusation single women often fend off. Or I've lucked into married couples who have married late, who have experienced the tension of waiting until marriage for sex and who know from experience that marriage doesn't automatically come with a college diploma. And over the years I've gotten pickier about who I choose as doctors. I am one for female gynecologists, especially for women who are virgins. I don't do this just out of modesty. I have found that female doctors are generally kinder to celibate women.

Some single women reason that if they can't have children, they can at least be around them. One way to ease the pain of unfulfilled maternal instinct is to offer to take care of married friends' kids for an evening or an afternoon, freeing up the weary parents. I tend to have friends who can't afford babysitters, so I've been known to show up on peoples' doorsteps on anniversaries and inform them that they are to take off for a few hours while I stay with the children. Thus, they get a break and I get my "fix" of kids that is enough to last me for weeks. This kind of service to our brothers and sisters in Christ would eliminate the accusation that singles are selfish and that we don't understand the problems of people with small children.

It helps to make our needs for affection known to our married friends who need to be reminded that the softest thing in our beds is our pillows. I need to be touched. One reason why singles feel unloved is because people rarely hug or touch them. I once told some friends that I hated sitting alone in church Sunday after Sunday. The married people were surprised to learn I felt that way, but they quickly picked up on what I had to say. The next Sunday, one of them was at my side right before the service, asking me to sit with him. The same thing happened the next Sunday.

And then there are the times when all the hugs, activities, and cold showers can't dispel our longings for sex. I've found it's best not to ignore these longings but to perceive the wellsprings of love and tenderness and giving that want to be expressed sexually. So I take certain factors involved in sex, such as being vulnerable and surrendered, and express them in a non-sexual way. I try to be honest with my feelings. I try to affirm people. I try to listen and talk less but say more. I try to avoid shrillness and bring forth firmness. I try not to complain—a big challenge. Bitterness, I've noticed, detracts from feminine graciousness.

Chervin notes that women give forth warmth whereas men emanate strength. So I work at being hospitable. Most days I choose skirts and dresses to wear to convey femininity; to play it up instead of down. Through trial and error, I've found it more advantageous to call tenderness and responsibility out of a man rather than put him on the defensive. These conclusions are not ones I have arrived at easily but are the product of what nearly a decade as a single career woman has taught me. And like Mary at the wedding at Cana, I've learned there is much to be said for the act of expressing the need at hand to her Son, then letting matters rest in his hands. Here again, that quality of surrender mixed with faith is required. But when truly exercised, it works. I've been in interviews or crowd situations where I've asked the Lord to bring me to certain people because I couldn't find them—and he did. This principle of surrender—in the right circumstances—is key to developing a healthy female sexuality.

God understands the single woman. The best statement I've ever read that expesses how he feels about us comes from poet Luci Shaw in her poem, "A Celibate Epiphany."

An apple is meant to be
flower & food & tree
& if it goes to rot, what
of its destiny?
      See,
here is a woman, planned
to be manned:
lover & mother
Single, she
is other
knowing only a kind
      of atrophy
(even an apple's designed

to be admired & eaten
    & climbed)
and who but God
    can exorcise
    the trauma
Of her empty thighs?
Between his palms dance
he twirls her brittle stem
    His fingers
Touch her virgin hem.
    His light shines,
    lingers,
    all glories glance
upon her inward parts.
    His purpose finds
    her heart of hearts,
    conceiving Jesus
    at her core
    by his most
Holy Ghost. Once more,
as with lonely Mary, he
    makes of her,
    in her own time
& in his time, his sweet
    bride, also a tree
thick enough to climb
    with petals
for the eye's delight
    and fruit to eat.

SIX

Sex and the Single Christian Man

I WAS IN CHURCH THE OTHER NIGHT watching a teenage boy try to decide whether he would acknowledge God or man. The occasion was a time of worship and three of his teenage friends sat to his left in the pew. A lot of people were lifting their hands in response to the beautiful song but he hesitated. I could see the wheels turning in his mind: what if his friends thought he was stupid? Or a fanatic? But he slowly got to his feet, closed his eyes and, as we began another stanza, raised one palm toward the ceiling.

It takes a real man to be open to God in front of others, whether that includes kneeling, responding to an altar call, or raising one's hands. These days, the test of manhood has changed from its former arena of winning battles and embarking on perilous journeys to either sports or the bedroom. For many men, sex is where they want to make the conquests that will give them bragging rights. It is status. Even for Christian men, who know quite well that premarital sex is wrong, some sort of light—or not-so-light—sexual play short of intercourse is often sought after.

But real manhood has nothing to do with the bedroom. It is personified in people like Hugh Latimer, an Anglican bishop who was martyred at the stake in 1555 by the forces of Bloody Mary. As the fires were being lit, he cried to his companion,

73

"Be of good comfort, Master Ridley, and play the man, and we shall this day light such a candle by God's grace in England as I trust shall never be put out."

Manhood is also John Milton, the English poet who wrote *Paradise Lost*. As a young man, Milton dreamed of writing a great Christian epic to make England preeminent in literature. But other involvements delayed him and in the prime of his life he became blind. In spite of that obstacle, he produced literature the world will never forget.

And it is Father Damien deVeuster, a Belgian priest who devoted his life to working with lepers on a Hawaiian island in the nineteenth century until he contracted leprosy and died of it. And it is Francis Schaeffer, who despite cancer, worked far past the time he should have retired. He was active in the fight against abortion and for the transformation of western culture back to a Christian world view until he died in 1984.

What manhood is not is pressuring women to comply physically with the man's wishes. Recently, I was reporting on a large religious convention where I became acquainted with another Christian reporter, a married man. We really clicked and at first I chalked up his affectionate gestures as being brotherly. But I wised up quickly when these gestures grew more intense as the convention progressed and I realized how inappropriate he was acting. Especially when he was always advising me to relax after telling me I appeared tense. Well, most reporters are tense while churning out two or three stories a day during a convention. Women get wary of a man telling them to relax, because we know they have ideas on how we can do it.

Or, the pressure is more subtle, such as the time I was coming home from an evening out and my companion made it plain he wanted more than a goodnight hug. Finally, "Don't you believe in romance?" he asked me. I resented being made to appear dull and boring. But I began to wonder if I was really normal, so I called my older brother Rob, who had experienced plenty of life before he married and eventually became a born-again Christian as he was entering his thirties. I asked him if I was missing the boat by not giving my date a kiss goodnight when to my mind a kiss signaled more serious intents than I cared to express.

"Well," replied my brother, "if you don't keep something in reserve, you'll have nothing left to give. People kiss each other one minute and stab each other in the back five minutes later. You're okay."

I posed the same question to another male friend over dinner.

"Most men don't take a kiss very seriously," he said, "but women do. Follow your instincts."

For people to whom going to bed on the first date is the most natural thing to do, I must seem like an anachronism. I must be part of what a *Texas Monthly* magazine article called the No Generation: no drinking while driving, no drugs, no smoking, no buying *Playboy* at 7-Eleven, no caffeine, no driving without seatbelts, and no sex with strangers. To that I add no sex with friends. Well, I do drink coffee.

The author of the *Texas Monthly* article, David Seeley, graduated from high school in 1975, a year after I did. He wrote of the joys our generation knew of sexual freedom and how sweet life was until herpes followed by AIDS appeared on the scene in the mid-1980s. Now the new machismo, Seeley wrote, may be saying no. It takes courage to say no, to resist peer pressure, and to go against the crowd. Success is based on saying no instead of yes. Most people with any honor or virtue are those who have learned to say no. Moral courage separates the men from the boys. David had it when he challenged Goliath. Stephen had it when he challenged the Jewish religious leaders. Joshua had it when he led God's people into the Promised Land.

In this age of the anti-hero, moral courage and purity are rare qualities. Contrary to the popular notion that women prefer men who are best in bed, I've found that what attracts me is a man's spirituality: his love and adoration of the Lord, his time spent in prayer, his love of the Word of God. That man will get my respect. Too often, men look for my affection without gaining my respect and for me, the two are inseparable. Too many men lean on women for spiritual counsel because there are no men they trust.

Why aren't the men helping each other out spiritually? In my church experience, women endlessly meet with each other—or even with other men—for lunches, prayer groups, Bible studies and the like. We support each other on the phone. We cry on each other's shoulders. This is not so with men. Men's groups in most churches are slow in starting, inarticulate about mutual support on things that really matter, and fearful of real vulnerability. When Christian men want comfort, they often seek out another woman whereas the better thing to do would be to develop strong relationships with men. Like women, men need spiritual bonding. Unlike women, they don't make time for it. Married men often have little energy after their job, wife, and kids to make room for such friendships, which is a shame since they are in a key position to disciple the single men. And the single men who'd like these kind of friendships get rebuffed by the married men. One of my single male friends, a businessman in a Southern city who attends a fast-growing evangelical church, told me pride is the problem.

"Men don't want to be vulnerable," he said. "They want to compete. I don't have any close buddy who knows my innermost secrets which leaves me suppressing a lot because I am not sure people can handle them. I need someone to whom I am significant other than my computer and my cat."

Quite a few men are trapped in the netherworld of an unsure masculinity modeled in some churches. *Rocky Mountain News* religion writer Terry Mattingly wrote about a Denver Episcopal parish that imported several male role model types: a military officer, a seminary president, and a bank chief executive officer to tell parishioners about the importance of spirituality in their lives.

"I think men make time for the things they care about," Mattingly quoted the parish priest as saying. "They will find the time to go goose hunting or play basketball, or play golf, or go see the [Denver] Bronco game.... Those are things men are supposed to do. But our culture says men aren't supposed to be part of spirituality and something that may affect your emotions, like the church, because that's supposed to be feminine somehow.... Many men don't feel comfortable on their knees. They just can't seem to submit, even to God."

Thus, they'll hardly submit to God's commands either. Bob Barnes, executive director of Sheridan House for Boys in Ft. Lauderdale, said that boys have been expected—by their parents no less—to lose their virginity sometime before marriage as proof of their potency and manhood. This had not been so with their daughters until recently. But now society says that neither men nor women should stay chaste until marriage. Barnes sees some reform coming with certain parents teaching their sons about staying chaste before marriage. But I'm afraid there's little talk of biblical figures, like Joseph, who landed in jail because he resisted the seduction attempts of Potiphar's lusty wife. These days, Joseph would be called a wimp for not following the woman into bed (unless, of course, she had AIDS).

We're so hardened. When a man chooses to stay a virgin, the world assumes he is gay. The possibility of a virile man making this choice is hardly thought of, really; not much literature exists on female virginity and male virginity is virtually ignored. The assumption is that there is nothing to write about.

When we see or hear of that kind of man, it's like listening to a voice from another age. Take Jim Elliot who, said his wife, Elisabeth, put off marriage and sex for five years while he established a place as a missionary in the Ecuadoran jungles. Now this was a man. In his twenties, he was writing entries in his journal such as, "Only I know that my own life is full. It is time to die, for I have had all that a young man could have, at

least all that this young man can have. I am ready to meet Jesus.
... God, I pray Thee, light these idle sticks of my life and may I
burn for Thee. Consume my life, my God, for it is Thine. I seek
not a long life, but a full one, like You, Lord Jesus."

Today, his dedication and singlemindedness are unparal-
leled. Elisabeth noted his strength early on in their relationship. "I wanted to marry a man prepared to swim against
the tide," she wrote in *Passion and Purity*. "I took it for granted
that there must be a few men left in the world who had that
kind of strength." Although the two didn't kiss for the first
time until he asked her to marry him, this apparently didn't
diminish their wedding night by one iota. As Elisabeth
succinctly wrote, "It was worth the wait."

Recently, I chanced upon an interview with Viv Grigg, a
New Zealand missionary profiled in the *City Watch* newsletter
from the Institute of Global Urban Studies in Pasadena,
California. This unusual man was trying to get commitments
from single Christians to remain single for five years so they
could live in the world's worst slums and so reach the teeming
millions there with the gospel. He had lived in Filipino slums
since the 1970s—hardly the Yuppie goal in life. He said, "If
the kingdom of God is to be established among the poor, there
must be a grain of wheat that dies amongst them, in order that
the fruit may come." And Grigg is such a grain of wheat.

The more typical Christian male lives in a gray world
described by Tim Larrick in the notorious spring, 1981 "sex
issue" published by the satirical evangelical Christian magazine *The Wittenburg Door*. In the article "Waterbed Wit-
nessing," Larrick wrote, "I certainly haven't figured out how
the definitive single Christian male should behave in regards
to premarital sex. Most of those to whom I have spoken about
this confusion have dealt with the issue themselves by getting
married." The alleged inability for men to exercise self-control
is just that—alleged. Society assumes that a man is sexually
healthy if he marries early. A marriage based on the man's
inability to put off sex may not be a stable marriage and his

wife may not have been the best woman for him. But he couldn't wait.

My married Christian friends tell me they can't imagine the agony of being single. Since nearly every male who teaches in a church is a married man, chastity is hardly a burning issue in most congregations. For many teenage boys, church is far removed from reality. "Sexual pressure," my brother Stephen wrote me, "is the stuff of youth. I think high school guys always want to believe that the best-looking girls are sexually active. I was intimidated by that ... I think you should remind us all that sexual taunts and challenges are just one part of the absurd cruelty that flourishes in high school. Guys push guys to extremes because they want vicarious thrills and better stories to tell."

A college friend told me that since men consider themselves the initiators of sex, they aren't taught how to separate sex from their sexuality.

"When I went to college, the question was always, 'How far did you get on your first date?' " he told me. "If you didn't have sex, you weren't being forward enough or you didn't have it. If we abstained, we were perceived as asexual." Not self-controlled, mind you, but backwards or out of it. People look to experience to define who they are, my friend added. The lack of sexual experience presupposes impotence. The church needs to support men at that point. Even if you've never kissed a woman, you're still a man. A man's sexual identity, from the start, depends on exploration and initiative, not sexual performance.

Another friend living in the Midwest said he used to work with men whose primary goal in life, as far as he knew, was to have sex with a different woman every night. They would taunt him, he said, suggesting he was either gay, didn't have a nice enough car, wasn't hanging around the right nightspots, and always the "if you don't use it, you'll lose it" line.

In early 1987, syndicated columnists Cheryl Lavin and Laura Kevesh published a column on male virgins. They had first run a story about female virginity, but got mostly responses from men in their twenties and thirties "who are also saving themselves," the women wrote. "And each one is sure he's the only one there is." One of the men they quoted said he found women to be the aggressors, making him feel guilty and unmasculine for not giving in. Men, they said, tend to be more misunderstood than women when they decide to wait until marriage for sex.

Today's "crisis of masculinity" shows little sign of lessening. Women's and men's roles have reversed; whereas the woman has moved out of the home, the man has moved further in. Magazines cover female sexual prowess as well as men's. With women becoming more aggressive, men either opt for super-macho or passivity.

Boston Globe columnist David Wilson described the dilemma of today's pre-teen boy who gets brought up in daycares, is rarely or never disciplined by his father, and many times doesn't have a father to emulate. In the past, when children underwent a long period of formation under stable parents, the typical boy learned not to put his elbows on the table, to do chores and homework, never to start a fight nor run away from one, and to prepare himself for the responsibility and authority of manhood. Whether or not this worked out, society agreed that this was how things were done. Today, such training for manhood is neglected. The breadwinning responsibility in a household often goes to the woman: the man has been displaced. He no longer has the authority he once had. Society has succeeded in abolishing childhood, Wilson says; it may abolish manhood next.

Black men are in worse shape, reports syndicated black columnist William Rasberry. Female students outnumber men four to one on most black college campuses and every time he speaks on one, several black women approach him to ask to be introduced to marriageable black men. But he has none to refer them to.

"Black men are fast becoming an endangered species," he

once wrote. "The bulk of young, black men are unskilled and jobless and are in no position to marry. Nevertheless, they do father children, but they don't contribute to families. So, they are perennially rootless and more often than not end up dead or in jail."

"Their children," Rasberry continued, "growing up in fatherless households, miss out on the things that fathers traditionally have provided: income, discipline and male role models. Again, it hits the boys the hardest. The young girls can learn something of what being a woman is about from their hard-pressed mothers. The boys are left to learn the lessons of manhood from that worst of teachers: the street."

The luckiest and brightest of the girls may stay in school and eventually land in middle-class careers, he reports, but the boys aren't taught the disciplines that middle-class children take for granted: setting goals, rigorous academics, and the post-ponement of sexual activity (or at least parenting) until after college.

Apparently churches aren't changing these standards much, at least among a group of 154 Houston teenagers, most of them black and Baptist, who were surveyed in early 1987. Although 63 percent of these teenagers said they attended church once a week, 67 percent of the boys and 39 percent of the girls thought premarital sex was okay. The median age that the boys wanted to start having sex was fifteen; the girls wanted to wait until seventeen. When asked who they would talk with should they have a sexual problem, boys listed church members last out of seven categories. Girls listed church members next to last.

The problem, said Richard Rohr, is that churches present youngsters with the choice of licentiousness or legalism. Forced to choose one, teenagers see no reason why they should wait for sex. And churches don't pound home the point that boys are perfectly capable of controlling their sexual desires. More often they lecture girls that it is their job to set the moral level of the relationship because the boys are supposedly helpless victims of their own hormones. In some cases, these same girls are taught to submit to men, and these men take advantage of that compliance by requesting sex. Match an uncontrolled boy with a compliant girl and the result is sexual disaster. Unfortunately, it is the woman who bears the brunt for sexual sin. She's the one who gets shunned if pregnant, and she must make those horrendous decisions about abortion and adoption.

Ideally, single men should plug into a Christian group that defuses their sexual desires, "but with most men, I find it is either all or nothing," Rohr said. "They either avoid women and they're afraid of women altogether or it's immediately an erotic sexual relationship. There's no ground in between. That's the sickness of the world. What's sad is how much we [Christians] have sold out to that."

Recently, I discovered a most intriguing book that addresses this problem, called *Men and Marriage* by George Gilder. It's an expanded edition of Gilder's 1973 book *Sexual Suicide*. Gilder sees the linchpin of civilization as being the willingness of men and women to lay down their lives for each other and for the mutual preservation of society: the man to work, the woman to raise children. What has made this century unique, says Gilder, is that the sexes have switched roles. Gilder argues that men are in essence "sexual barbarians": chaotic and destructive creatures who need marriage to channel them into a lasting and productive way of life, namely the family. Nearly all successful men are married men, he says, and single men often show little sustained commitment and a lack of planning for the future. He adds that marriage, unlike singleness, is made to bear the impact of children. The result is civilization. Traditionally, a woman persuaded a man to channel his energies into a home and family by agreeing only to have sex with him within marriage. Thus, man got his sexual fulfillment, woman also got her sexual needs met plus a stable environment where she could raise their children. Women civilize men by marrying them. In spite of its imperfections, civilization has existed on this social reality up until now, Gilder says.

But the sexual revolution, with its contribution of sex apart from marriage, changed it all, he declares. It freed men from having to marry, but brought back man as the sexual barbarian: the playboy and cruiser. Women now sell their sexual birthright by settling for sex before marriage, thus eliminating man's major reason to marry. Why should they? A host of abnormalities have resulted: low birth rates, no-fault divorce, single parenthood, safe sex, the acceptance of gay lifestyles as normal, and a high abortion rate. The removal of sexual restrictions has brought sexual competition, not liberation. And so the family slowly crumbles.

Eddie Hernandez, a pastor I came to know while living in Miami, places the blame on the breakup of the family and the sexual activity of the young on the "uncaring, unthinking and uncommitted parents. It is amazing how often the Scriptures speak of the role of the father in the upbringing of the family. Today, coveting has made both father and mother non-existent in the family unit. Things have become more important than family."

Edwin Louis Cole, a Dallas pastor who stages conventions and meetings for men only, writes that one of his biggest tasks is getting men to simply forgive their fathers. Only God can heal some of those disastrous relationships, he says, but it is clear that a sinful father can sour a son permanently on God. Cole gets around the bitterness sons feel about this by insisting they are responsible for their lives, no matter what their parents did.

"Maturity doesn't come with age, it comes with the acceptance of responsibility," he wrote in *Courage: A Book for Champions*. Elsewhere, he adds, "Thank God there are young men who have that burning desire to be outstanding . . . men who are willing to pay the price for the true manhood which is Christlikeness . . . single men who realize they need to grow and mature as men now, not waiting until they are married."

SEVEN

Between 10 P.M. and 2 A.M.

I WAS BUMMING A RIDE HOME after work from another reporter one day when we started talking about men. Since her divorce, she had been sleeping around somewhat.

"I can't imagine not doing it at all," she admitted. "I mean, once you've been through all those years of marriage, who's to care whether you've slept with one person or three? I've got my needs and I need them met every so often. Those desires don't stop right when the marriage does."

"You mean," I said, "once you get a divorce, then there's no reason to not sleep with someone else?"

"That's right," she said, while steering her car through rush hour traffic. "To not have sex at all? I'm not a nun. I can't imagine an existence like that."

I've heard the same message from other divorced female friends: Christian and non-Christian. Used to frequent sex in marriage, they don't feel the urgency of remaining chaste, as they did when they were virgins. It's like an oven: once the pilot light is turned on, bringing on the heat takes much less effort. But just as sex is a habit that takes getting used to, so is celibacy. John White calls this "sexual fasting."

Sexually experienced or not, the hardest time of the day for any normal single person is between 10 P.M. and 2 A.M., when, we presume, much of humanity is enjoying sex. We flip through books and magazines, toss, turn, watch TV, pray, read the Bible, read the comics, count sheep, and muster up other ways to deal with our aloneness.

Of all the topics that so desperately need to be discussed and dealt with among Christians, sexual desires head up the list. Everyone has them but no one discusses them. When is the last time we've spoken up during prayer time at the weekly Bible study group to ask for help in battling lust? The only forum in which I can imagine this is among singles, since it is next to impossible for most married couples to identify with us. The worst types among them are those who, after having been separated from their spouses after a two-week business trip, feel they now understand the pains of celibacy. They've only played at celibacy. Delayed gratification is different than the prospect of no gratification at all. In some ways, their empathy can be a disservice to us: because they can't imagine a life without sex, they are reluctant to wish that on us. It is reassuring Christ did without it, and he didn't suffer any harmful effects from that lack.

We must face our sexuality head-on, instead of avoiding it, repressing it, or labeling it as sinful. There is no virtue in simple avoidance, which is nigh impossible anyway.

When the *Chronicle* did an article on the newest fashions in seductive high school prom dresses, one fashion designer attributed the popularity of the sexy strapless, off-the-shoulder, and halter-top dresses in black metallic lame, crinoline, satin, and taffeta to the pop star Madonna. These senior girls weren't snatching anything in muslin or dotted swiss off the racks. At every turn, we're hit with the message that sex appeal—even in clothing—leads to ultimate ful-fillment and is necessary for a balanced life.

On the other hand, married friends will inform us that the process can be a drag and that we should never marry on the basis of sex alone.

"Television," one of my brothers wrote me, "warps all our expectations. So much of the whole bedroom adventure is awkward, sloppy, embarrassing. You're revealing so much to someone: the extra flab around your tummy, the quality of your patience, the extent of your selfishness, the laundering of your sheets. You have to ask yourself, 'Why?' One hopes the whole experience will remain slightly intimidating to protect the romantics who launch into all this expecting a cinematic event to rival the best moments of *About Last Night* or *Children of a Lesser God*."

Christians don't have a corner on sexual control. Ultra-Orthodox Jews have a system by which they literally apply Old Testament law to their sex lives: men are not supposed to have sex with their wives for the length of her menstrual period and the seven days that follow. During this period of abstinence, many Orthodox couples sleep in separate beds. Only after the wife immerses herself in a *mikveh*—a ritual bath—on the eve of the seventh day can the couple resume sexual relations. This might seem like a great hardship but the two-week hiatus was refreshing and needed by the Orthodox women I interviewed. These women happily embraced the practice. The enforced abstinence was seen as a great boon to their sex lives during the remaining eighteen-or-so days of the month. With a shortened amount of time available, couples got less bored with each other and were less apt to make up excuses about not having sex. Delayed gratification worked wonders. And judging from the customary large families in a typical Orthodox household, the practice didn't curtail fertility, either. Their method of separation proved to me that our supposedly uncontrollable sexual urges can be regimented to a great extent in obedience to a higher law. The Orthodox cheerfully put up with this for the sake of the Torah, the first five books of the Bible.

Once I was interviewing Sheina Koenigsburg, the heroine of the book *Holy Days* by Lis Harris. The book is about the ultra-Orthodox Lubavitch movement in Judaism to which Koenigsburg belongs. After she described to me the strict separation of sexes that begins in elementary school among Lubavitch children, she added that the group avoids teenage suicide, teenage pregnancy, drugs, AIDS, and a host of other ills.

"There seems to be something positive in our lifestyle," she told me, "because our community (in Brooklyn Heights, N.Y.) is growing by leaps and bounds. The Torah was given to all the Jews. If anybody has deviated, it is they who have left the Torah."

The best way to understand a desire is often not to give in to it. I better understand food cravings now that I've been a Weight Watchers member for eleven years. Now I can control how I eat; before, I could not. The ability to be thin is a daily choice that begins the night before when I make up my bag lunch (and breakfast and dinner on a busy day). We make sexual choices the same way by not putting ourselves in positions where we get tempted or where we are too vulnerable. For instance, alcohol can lower inhibitions. If we are drunk or sleepy, we are not in control. Anyone who wants to remain chaste must keep their wits about them. Too many men and women have lost their virginity while drunk at some party. In fact, it's an immense education to stay sober at a party where everyone else is drunk. You develop a sense of distance quickly. When we are not alert, it is too easy to land in the back seat of a car or in a back bedroom.

We've been brainwashed into thinking that we shouldn't impose any restraints on our sexual desires. Denying sexual feelings is not healthy, but abstinence never hurt anyone. If periods of sexual abstinence can refresh and renew a marriage, there's no truth to the thought that the body must continually have sex. The body does what we tell it to do. I should know: I've made mine jog ten kilometers in races and it's made it past the finish line. Sexual expression in marriage is one expression of the human personality. When this expression is blocked, we can wallow in misery or choose other outlets: intercession, graduate level study, artistic creativity, or service to the poor.

It seemed logical to me when I've approached my thirties, a time when a woman's sexual capacities are at her peak, I've been drawn to lengthy periods of intercessory prayer and some fasting. I was twenty-eight when I felt called to make some sacrifices in order to see revival and renewal spring forth in my church. So I organized a group of people to fast one day a week for certain intentions. I don't especially enjoy fasting and I find it uncomfortable as well as unglamorous. But I poured a lot of energy into that prayer effort during the eight months we prayed for renewal. I feel we accomplished something for the kingdom of God. Soon after I moved to Texas, I organized a similar effort at intercession on a smaller scale. I think we need to give out in some way; if not sexually, then elsewhere. This is a way of surrendering our sexual desires to God, which does wonders for breaking the powerhold that sex has over us. It amazes me to realize the highly-charged energy that single people have available for the Lord, but it saddens me to see how little of it is used for his purposes. Perhaps we secretly fear that if we use it for him, we'll retain none for ourselves in case we ever need it. But Christ challenges us to give, and as we give, he'll keep our supplies full. We who have strong sexual desires should never feel condemned because the strongly sexed can strongly serve.

God is no fool when it comes to sex and he welcomes our thoughts on it—or how we wish we had it. He can handle our honesty, pain, and anger, but he cannot tolerate our deceit. He's not afraid of our feelings, but be forewarned: he'll lob back some surprising answers. Gutsy prayers get gutsy answers and one comeback he's tossed my way is that he certainly knew sexual temptation on earth and understands my longings. This was hard for me to grasp; after all, he was not a woman, but it occurs to me that I underestimate his capacity to feel my pain.

Unfulfilled sexual desires are such a source of pain that we often feel it simpler to deny them altogether. As Christians, we choose not to give in, but there's a danger in turning off our feelings altogether. This can kill all tenderness in us. Instead of being submitted to Christ, who makes us face our pain, we choose the Law in a sense. A case in point are people who, in a church that allows brotherly-sisterly hugs and simple gestures of affection, refuse to touch anyone. They say they don't need the contact; what they're really afraid of is that they may cry. Or that they'll open themselves up too much to others and then not be able to withdraw. Another case are people who are so into self-control that they try to control others as well. Paradoxically, in vulnerability is our power. When we let others have at us at a level where they could hurt us if they chose, we lose the severity that denying our feelings brings. Repressed people are lonely, driven, controlling, and functional people. They cannot give out because they are not taking in. But those who surrender their sexuality to Christ find that he first demands we learn to adore him. That is step one in admitting that we are not sufficient and that he is greater. As we do so, he breaks us, kindly, to make us less brittle and more yielding. Our trust in him grows when we realize he won't hurt us. Then, feeling protected and secure in him, we give out. We don't need to erect walls because he is our shield.

A man who has spent long hours in private worship is John Michael Talbot, a lay Franciscan monk and Christian musician from Eureka Springs, Arkansas. In his book, *The Fire of God,* he describes how he has dealt with lust. Being divorced, he knew what he was giving up when he took on poverty, chastity, and obedience. He says that praise, a healthy asceticism (such as fasting, self-denial, and a simple lifestyle), praying in tongues, and allowing himself to weep are helpful. I agree. Praise, however unwilling I feel about it, gets my mind off myself. Once a week, I attend a 5:30 A.M. prayer meeting at my church. We have learned to enjoy worshipping the Lord at such an hour, even though most of us are hardly awake enough to pray, much less sing. We more often croak along. This is a form of discipline and self-denial, of sleep if nothing else. Although I have to be up at 4:30 A.M. to dress and drive sixteen miles to that meeting, it is always worth it.

Fasting, as hard as it is, yields good fruit. I feel more spiritually sharp—on the cutting edge as it were—after having done so. I feel as though I've chucked some excess baggage. I wait for a divine nudge to fast because doing so merely for dietary reasons puts me in a rotten mood. I can't last out the day. If I sense God wants me to fast for whatever reason, then the motivation is there to stick it out.

I agree with Talbot that when desires or feelings overwhelm us and we must express our perplexity to God, it helps to pray in tongues. We need to give voice to our deepest longings, especially when we don't know how to describe what those longings are. That form of prayer is cleansing, but risky, as it creates within us a certain brokenness and humility before God. We really are pouring out our hearts to him. This is what he wants: that we communicate with him in our worst conditions as well as our best. As we gaze at him, we are changed from glory to glory.

Another way to avoid lust and sexual problems is to bring order into our lives. If our room, desk, and schedule are all disasters, chances are that we'll have disorder in our sexuality. As we set in order the other parts of our lives, sometimes our sexual desires will dissipate. Then there's exercise. Some of my friends find great relief from sexual stress in jogging or swimming. These activities either drain us physically or pep us up, so we each need to find what works for us. It helps to take monthly rhythms into account here, especially women whose sexual highs and lows vary according to their menstrual cycle. Often, women feel the most desire during certain times of their cycle. Anticipating these difficult times before they arise helps us to recognize them for what they are and wait them out.

Sometimes our lifestyle is too pressured: too much to do, perform, complete. We give into masturbation, pornography, fantasy, or sex itself as a way of letting off steam. Some of us live inside our heads too much. We are overly introspective and easily depressed. Sometimes that comes from not enough interaction with people; other times it comes from boredom.

Pornography has been described as a fear of relationships. Pornography is a vicarious relationship wherein one can experience fulfillment, albeit a false fulfillment, without the give and take and suffering love of a real relationship. Masturbation also eliminates the bother of having to deal with another human being. John White says masturbation's major defect is that it aborts what was meant to be a powerful urge for intimate relationships. That which was meant to be shared, he writes in *Eros Defiled*, is squandered in solitude. Part of the reason for sex is to know and be known. Masturbation doesn't do that. I remember talking with a Christian friend in Oregon who was describing some counseling she was getting. She admitted that at the root of her sexual confusion was her struggle over masturbation. This wasn't something she was particularly happy about, she said, adding that the practice was dragging her down spiritually.

The gamut of sex-and-single-Christians books that mention masturbation are divided on the subject. Scripture offers no direct insight on the matter. Some say it is better to masturbate than to have premarital sex, if one must choose one way or another. Some say to avoid it because it leads to fantasizing. Some say it doesn't glorify God, which is my stance. Instead of diffusing sexual tension as some claim, masturbation increases desire. Once at a college Christian retreat, the whole group of us was floored when one of the upper classmen confessed he had a problem with masturbation and asked for prayer. None of us despised the guy; instead, we admired him for having the guts to admit to something no doubt many of the students in that room struggled with.

One male friend told me that he is not up to the constant mental battle that abstinence from masturbation demands. For him, it is either fornication or masturbation.

"Given my circumstances, it's the best thing I can do," he said. "I'm not proud of it. I wish I could have asked more men about it, but it's a taboo topic."

Whenever I am faced with a questionable sexual practice, I ask myself the crude but apt question: would Jesus have done it? The answer becomes clearer. No.

The problem is twofold: the desires that come from our bodies and the thoughts that spring from our minds. It's no accident that people say the brain is the chief sex organ: that which we fantasize about, we often do. Fantasy is for me the thorniest of areas. Some Christian friends inform me they don't fantasize at all, which means they and I are on different planets where that is concerned. Perhaps such a state is possible. I have not reached it.

Years ago, I stumbled on some common-sense guidelines on fantasizing that have helped me:

—The Lord wants us to be the master (or mistress) of our desires, not their slave.

—Fantasies often only stimulate desires and leave us frustrated and depressed. Acknowledge them to be normal, then resist them as temptation.

—Figure out what stimulates wrong desires and avoid that.

—Resist thoughts that lead us to think of things that will probably never happen. Let the Lord rule your life instead of you planning things out.

—Be realistic. You may need to tell your thoughts no.

—Get things out in the light and talk about them with people you trust. Things look bigger in the dark.

—Fantasies take the surprise and pleasure out of the Lord's hands because we've already made the plans.

—God does not want us in bondage to anything. 1 Peter 1:13 says we are to gird our minds. God has given us the power to do this.

—Consider Psalm 63:6. Do we meditate on the Lord upon our beds or upon ourselves?

Sex is the force that feeds the flower of our youth. Either it will master us or we will master it. God has left that choice to us.

EIGHT

We Are the Family of God

IT WAS A HOT, BRIGHT, LUSH EASTER that year, a day of pageantry, music, and incense at my church. I was feeling secure and loved: after all, I had a place to go after the service. A young couple had invited me to share their Easter dinner along with their two children, as my family was three thousand miles away.

Immediately after the service the wife approached me with a look on her face that made my heart sink. She said her husband had decided that because his parents were coming over, they simply couldn't accommodate me, too. I was left standing in the middle of the parking lot as car after car pulled away. It was too late to invite myself elsewhere. So I spent the afternoon alone. The one consolation was that I had a barbeque to go to that night at the home of another church member. I often counter loneliness by inviting others over, but it has been my experience that singles have to do 80 percent of the initiating. Inviting a single person over to lunch is not a high priority for most married couples. So we're on our own here.

Nothing hits the single Christian—or single anyone for that matter—harder than the holidays. As I've moved about the country and away from my family, I've grown to dislike holidays intensely. Our self-esteem rises and falls depending on whether we get invited anywhere, and thus every Mother's

Day, Easter, Thanksgiving, and Christmas is painful. I never know where I am going to spend them. Like many singles, I hesitate to invite myself anywhere for fear the host or hostess won't want me.

Foreseeing this, some churches organize splashy singles events for the holidays so at least the singles can be with each other. But many of us don't want more activities. One of the big myths of the church is that singles only want to be with each other. Most singles I know would junk a singles lunch any day to spend the afternoon with a family. Families may think they have little time as it is for themselves, much less time for a guest, so it takes us awhile to get across to people that, like Jesus with Mary and Martha, all we want is them, not their polished dinner service. While living in South Florida, I used to spend time with a couple from church who had three small girls whose mission in life was to make sure I got my quota of hugs and kisses for the month. I just loved being there, even if I had to step over a pile of laundry to get into the bathroom. There was a lot of light and love there. I miss them.

We singles want family, not a singles group. I enjoy being invited to people's homes, not just on holidays when people are feeling dutiful, but during evenings and especially on Sunday afternoons, my loneliest times. Why are singles the last to leave church on Sunday mornings? Because they have nowhere else to go. My single male friends especially resent the artificial separation of people into groups of singles and marrieds—kind of like have-nots and haves—at church. The church is the only institution I can think of that does this. Wearing a wedding ring does not change one's spirituality. Many churches reinforce this impression by appointing only married couples to head Sunday school classes, house churches, and the like. One spiritually mature friend was passed over for a leadership position simply because he was not a married man. The singles ministry in his church is mainly geared towards preparing for marriage.

In our task-oriented society, marriage is considered the

norm by church leaders, even though Christianity's founder was a single man. Recently, I stopped by a large evangelical Houston church to buy a collection of tapes on singleness to give to a friend. When he opened it, we both laughed: one of the tapes was on sex, the other three were on preparing for marriage. The best churches are where the individual is a member of a family, not a social club. For us singles, church is one of the few social places we can go without someone demanding sex from us. If we want a club, we know how to find many flashier places that serve that function better than a church.

A church needs to do what it does best: be the family of God. Within families, people generally trust each other. The relationships are permanent and they don't stop if members get mad at each other. Our culture says the individual is whole. Christianity says that the community is whole, that we find ourselves (in relationship) as we deal with each other. This is true: when I'm alone reading a magazine at home, I don't grow a whole lot in a spiritual sense. When I'm tussling some matter out with a friend at church, especially when we disagree strongly, I grow a lot. People sharpen each other.

This is a more painful route. It is easier to choose a dead church, where no commitment—or maybe the most shallow-kind—is asked of us. Or we can remain anonymous in a life-giving church so that the truly important things remain unsaid and the vital questions remain unasked. So many of us in large cities who are hundreds if not thousands of miles away from our families need our brothers and sisters in Christ to truly act the part, to be our advisors, confidants, and family.

Some singles who've been burned before in church opt out of more commitment. One single male Christian friend of mine rarely attends church because of his disillusionment with past fellowships. When he does go, he attends a spiritually dead congregation where he doesn't have to reveal much of himself. And that choice has stunted him spiritually. Rarely does he mention the Lord or give some indication of an ongoing relationship with him. Paradoxically, when we choose to interact with other Christians, something of Christ rubs off on us. We all grow together far faster than separately. Sometimes singles stay away from heavy involvement with a church because they are sexually active and they know their church friends would frown on that. But generally, I've found that people want friendship more than churchiness. Church can be the place where we find real friends. But if we don't find spiritual love in the church, we short-circuit that by resorting to sex.

The major responsibility for singles is to go to the church, not where the best-looking potential mates are necessarily, but where God calls us. And he will call us to a certain place. In the last two cities I've lived in, my congregation has not been the magnet church in the region for singles. Yet, I've been called to those places. And friends who attend those magnet churches report back that there are many people in line ahead of them, most of them women, all going for a small number of available men. Often being committed to a particular church takes all the faith and hope we can muster. It is far easier to stay home and switch on a TV evangelist or head for the beach. Where faith and hope aren't demanded of us, deep love becomes impossible. Church, I've found, is like a marriage. We make that commitment, then stick with it despite all temptations to move on to greener pastures.

The choice of the right church is a serious one that should not be rushed into. But it needs to be made as soon as practically possible. In Miami, I took one month to decide on a church. In Houston, I took six weeks. After finding a roommate and a place to live, church has been my third priority. A sure way to cure those newcomer blues is to join a church—fast.

Many of us may be in the wrong churches, especially those that promote alienation instead of family. The last three I've belonged to were family-like. All three included "house churches," otherwise known as agape groups, shepherd groups, home fellowships, neighborhood groups, cell groups, and other designations. They are a product of the 1970s, which is when people realized that churches need to cater to the individual as well as the corporate. The world's largest church in Seoul, South Korea, grew to its present size through house churches. Under a house church system, congregations are divided largely by geographical area into smaller units that meet once a week between Sundays for worship, Bible study, and fellowship. These groups have been my lifeline for the past decade. We have cried together, prayed together, and shared our job woes and our successes with each other. We know each other's birthdays, problems, and families. True spiritual power grows out of this type of community because God seems to make us Christians more fruitful and we hear God's voice more clearly when we are together.

This came home to me recently when my parish stopped all church activities and meetings to have a vigil to discern our future direction as a church. For two hours a day, every day except Sunday, we sat in a darkened church and listened to the Lord speak to us individually. Then we met in small groups to share our findings. As we met, even in silence, simply being there knit us together. On the last night of the vigil, we had deep, heartfelt, intense worship together. But there would not have been such a celebration without the shared life of the previous two weeks.

People are searching for that kind of fulfillment and they will spend themselves in most amazing ways for the sake of the kingdom of God. A case in point are the 5:30 A.M. prayer meetings I've mentioned. If we didn't think God was hearing and answering our prayers there, we wouldn't come. Our church gives us our only sense of purpose we're likely to have outside of our workplaces. *The Wall Street Journal* ran a two-part series about the loneliness of American life, typified by Gwinnett County north of Atlanta. As of the spring of 1987, it was the fastest-growing county of more than 100,000 residents in the nation. It had held that distinction for three years.

Anchored more by Gwinnett Place Mall than by any civic building, it is a place without a soul, the article said. It is hard to get people involved in county affairs; residents took part in their homeowners' associations more than anything else and one observer described Gwinnett County as, "filled with a lot of people who drive alone to work and then drive home and turn on their VCRs." Another observer called such suburban cities "urbanoid villages" that deliver traffic, fail to deliver services, and fail miserably at any semblance of community. Not surprisingly, the county's churches are full, the article said. A friend of mine living in the area said his church is bursting at the seams with singles. Since singles are one of the hardest groups to get inside a church, the impersonal character of greater Atlanta must have been overwhelming enough to drive many of these singles to church in search of some connecting.

Will we find what we want when we get there? Free at last from the ties of our families and college life, the last thing a single person wants is accountability. Yet this is what we need in order to stay disciplined and spiritually fit. If we can't marry into a natural family, then we need to develop a spiritual family, such as those house churches where we can let our hair down. We are intimate with these people. These are the people we don't run away from. We share with the people there, we are dealt with and reformed. With them, we can be vulnerable, open, loving, and forgiving. We can take risks. Such groups are training grounds and places for constant fine-tuning. It is here that we hear the voice of the Lord corporately, since such groups are more flexible than the scenario at a typical Sunday morning service. It's important that such a group include at least one peer, which is a person on our spiritual level with whom we can relate as equals. If all the people in this group are light years ahead of us, we'll always feel inferior. If they are all spiritual babes whereas we are not, we'll be constantly drained. In American culture, the nuclear family is the only thing that even resembles the set-up I have described. But even that is incomplete because the husband and wife are of one flesh and the children are dependent persons. And a marriage where the husband and wife depend on each other for all their needs is an ingrown marriage.

We singles must seek out a spiritual family in the church to which God beckons us. It is no excuse to say we do not have the time. We must make the time. If anyone has had rat race jobs with long and crazy hours, it has been me in the last ten years. Yet, during my first three years as a reporter in Portland, Oregon, I lived two of those years in a community household. That was incredibly time-consuming because I had a lot of intense relationships happening at the same time. In recent years, I've invested significant amounts of free time in church activities instead of joining a running club, which I'd like to do. But I couldn't do both. Although I like to run, I feel that what goes on in church is more significant in an eternal sense than whether I can get my running time down to under an hour for ten kilometers. If we really believe that God has entrusted the salvation of the world and the preaching of the Great Commission into the hands of the church, we need to put our leisure time where it counts.

Sadly, many churches are nowhere near our wavelength. They are inarticulate when it comes to sexuality and sexual temptation and offer little or no support for maintaining chastity. But the church has also been criticized for concentrating too much on sexual sin to the exclusion of corporate sins such as the nuclear arms build-up. Despite this, sexual sin is as alive in the church as ever. No, I think churches talk about sexual sin, but give no believable alternatives to singles on how not to have sex. Although all sin is the same in the eyes of God, the effect of sexual sin is more catastrophic. Surrender to sexual sin defiles us in a way that, say, gluttony can never do. It wounds us to the cores of our beings. Paul points out in 1 Corinthians 6:18 that other sins affect us in an exterior sort of way; sexual sin alone is a deeper sin against our own bodies. This needs to be explained in a more understandable way for people who write off the church for being too puritanical about sex.

Sexuality is something we may rely on outside speakers to address over a singles weekend, but afterwards, we don't pick up the ball and run with it. Instead of going to non-Christian outlets to get solace, why not offer a Christian view of this most important part of our lives? Haven't we already done this with abortion: providing pregnancy clinics so that women considering an abortion can consider an alternative? For this to happen at church would require the delicacy and wisdom of a Solomon. It seems that organized classes on Christian sexuality could work best on a lecture format until participants grew comfortable enough with each other to share some of their thoughts. Since a typical forty-five-minute Sunday school class containing participants who see each other once a week isn't the best vehicle for revealing life's secrets, I'd suggest splitting discussion into very small groups that should probably be organized according to sex.

What needs to be conveyed to the church at large is the need for leadership to tackle this issue. People generally want to talk on these subjects but they have no graceful way to bring them up. The leaders of such a group would have to be levelheaded sorts who can be honest about their struggles with sexuality. If those people are nervous or uptight, discussion will die. One misconception that singles have is that once people are married, all sexual problems and temptations fade away. It was a real shock when a good married Christian friend told me (in front of his wife) that one of his biggest temptations was still pornographic magazines. A church forum on sexuality involving married people as well as singles can do a lot to eliminate the resentment singles often feel towards the married for being insensitive. One of the best conversations I've ever had on this topic was with a married couple involved with a youth ministry. They were used to dealing with sexual matters and they surprised me by admitting how difficult it had been for them to adjust to sex when they married. It was certainly not at all the careless, joyous event they had read about, they said, and getting used to each other sexually had taken them many months. And they knew of other married friends who were still struggling after two years. That one conversation eliminates some of my misconceptions about marriage.

Another helpful way churches can tackle sexual issues is to be real. Call a spade a spade. As a beginning reporter, I spent a lot of time poring over police reports, many of them searing accounts of sex crimes. Reporting on them was one part of my job I hated, but it did build in me a toughness about the slime in which so much of the world lives. I was confronted daily by reality. Then I'd go to church, which was like moving from *Miami Vice* to Disneyland. The atmosphere was so sweet that I wondered if anyone could understand the kind of people I read about in the crime reports.

"The church needs to speak to the fact that there are incest victims in the pews who can't remember a time when they weren't having sex," one reporter told me. "For them, 'no' may have become an impossible, undreamable word. They may think they're going to hell anyway so it doesn't matter. In a non-judgmental way, the church needs to help people like this build up the strength, the courage, and the knowledge to live in chastity. Just saying that fornication is a sin is not enough for some people."

Churches place great stress on the nuclear family while ignoring the fact that a growing percentage of their population in the pews is single. What is on the agenda of the typical church is not on the list of most interesting topics for the single person. I'd also suggest asking the singles in any church what they want to hear about, not what the leadership thinks they ought to hear. Many singles feel that the leadership has little to teach them about sex, and they need to be persuaded differently. Chances are that singles will come up with a much different list of wants than the menu they are currently being served. For instance, people assume that singles always want to go out and eat. They think we have a fixation on pizza. This gets old, especially for people trying to stay thin or keep within a tight budget. Church leaders make the same mistakes with singles that they do with youth: assume they want a never ending diet of amusements. The opposite is true: singles would rather discard the fluff of Christian concerts and campouts and get down to real things that demand sacrifice. People long for a challenge. Something in human spirits longs to sacrifice all to follow the Lord, provided they get spiritual power and meaning in return. But the choice must be clearly presented. We need to hear a call to duty and discipline, not on how to be Christian and Yuppie at the same time. As much as we run from hearing the message of the cross, we know we need to hear that the cross is the crux of our faith.

Churches need to recognize the things that are important to us. In both Christian and Jewish subcultures, marriage is celebrated. Singleness is not. One single woman in my church in Oregon threw a fiftieth birthday party for herself and invited the whole congregation. She said she wanted to celebrate who she was since by then it was obvious she would never marry. Singles don't receive the affirmation one gets from wedding and baby showers or bachelor parties. Marriage and children are rites of passage in our society and those of us who have neither miss out. My church in Miami threw me a wonderful going-away party before I moved to Houston. It was the first time outside of a birthday party that I had been the center of attention as an adult. Think of a creative occasion to honor the single person in your church.

Don't sound an uncertain note. Don't preach that fornication is evil, then allow an unmarried couple who is living together to have a leadership position in the church. One former pastor of mine was faced with such a couple who had no intention of foregoing sexual relations with each other. Since he knew his integrity was on the line, he advised them to repent. When they refused, he told them they were no longer welcome at our church. They promptly went to a nearby church where they were promoted to leadership while continuing to live together. Word of this spread throughout that congregation and the couple ended up poisoning that church. Disgusted with what they perceived as their pastor's lack of backbone, people left that church and came over to ours.

Don't talk doubletalk. People are quick to say, "We'll have you over sometime," but slow to make good on that promise. It may be hard for married couples to believe that we single people would want to come to a messy house full of noisy children, but many of us would enjoy this homey atmosphere. One of our greatest desires is to feel like we belong. Include us in family life. Let us know that our lives are interesting to married people. While you are showing us your baby pictures, remember to ask us about the things that fill our lives—our work and relationships. Draw us out by asking us questions. Let us know that we are worth listening to.

Get serious about attracting men. There's often nothing in the church for the masculine man looking for models he can relate to. Men often don't come to Christ because they see a church composed of women and for women. They fear the church will somehow emasculate them. Men whose identity is tied to their sex lives are at a loss if they can't have sex. Men need to be shown how they can be men without taking someone to bed. I'd love to see a church that took the needs of its single women seriously and made an effort to recruit men. Recently I've been getting mail from various Jewish organizations around the country describing the high rates of inter-marriage and the resulting loss to Judaism. Jewish women as well as Christian women are having trouble finding mates. The Jewish newspaper in Houston has started a section for singles and singles events to match Jews to other Jews. Would that Christians were as concerned about intermarriage between Christians and nonbelievers! It amazes me to see Christian men dating non-Christian women without a word of reproof from their elders in the church. The single Christian woman is left to her own devices and, if she wearies of waiting and marries a non-believing man, then she gets criticized for not waiting for a Christian mate.

Fill the simplest of needs like walking single women out to their cars and sitting with singles of either sex in church. Give them one of your children to hold. Married couples sail into the sanctuary with kids in tow: singles wander in furtively looking around for someone, anyone to sit next to. I still hate pausing those horrible ten or twenty seconds in the back of church, trying to recognize the backs of peoples' heads so I can find someone I know. In the past, I've sat alone for the first year in a church until I knew people well enough to risk rejection and ask if I might sit next to them.

Touch us. I've said this before, but it bears repeating. One reason why singles feel unloved is that we're rarely held or touched. Compare this with the behavior of your average married couple and notice how husbands and wives literally cling to each other. According to 1 Corinthians 7:4, they possess the rights to each other's bodies. Single people don't have that comfort. Church is the one place where celibates who long for sexual love can receive healthy love.

At my church in Houston, the ushers literally hug—or at least try to—everyone who comes through the front door. This really impressed a reporter I brought to church for the first time. After we were both warmly embraced at the front door, she remarked when we sat down, "You didn't tell me about those ushers." Later in the service, when it came time for everyone to exchange greetings, I reached out to shake her hand. But no, even that small greeting at the door had made its impact. She gave me a hug.

NINE

The New Virginity

ALTHOUGH EVERYONE HAS BEEN A VIRGIN, popular conceptions of virginity as a permanent state of being convey the freedom of a jail cell, the openness of a chastity belt, and the joy of a hair shirt. Its exclusiveness makes for dull dinner discussions. Its possibilities are unexplored for the fear it may be catching.

When 1 Corinthians 6:20 says we were bought with a price, therefore we should glorify God with our bodies, this includes saving ourselves for marriage. And if we do not marry, we then save ourselves for God. Many of us are waking up to this second reality, yet few of us understand how to live out a life without sex.

We worry whether the wait will spoil us for the pleasure we hope to experience when we do marry. However, sexual power is not dissipated when it is controlled. When a river flows through a narrow canyon, its power is not lost. Instead, it is enormously increased by the narrow restraint. If we give away our virginity before marriage, we steal from the intensity and wonder of early married sexuality. That first awkwardness is a small price to pay for the knowledge that we bestowed a priceless gift on our mate. We must understand that real love is restrained and controlled. Real love says no before marriage. And Scripture makes it clear that sexual consummation is saved for marriage just as dessert, so to speak, is saved until the last. It's interesting that Leviticus 21:7, 13-15 specifies that a

Levite high priest, a man holy to the Lord, is required to marry a virgin. Would that all single men considered themselves just as holy.

There's been little emphasis on the priceless quality of virginity even in the church. Deep down inside, people realize its value, but we give it away on a whim or because of an unwillingness to be different. Often, we trade it off for something worthless, like Esau selling his birthright for a bowl of lentils. And we only give away our sexual purity once. I heard a poignant anecdote on this matter during a *Focus on the Family* radio show with California pyschologist Dr. James Dobson and Elisabeth Elliot. She was recalling a large singles conference at which she spoke where a young man told her he had just discovered his fiancée was not a virgin. Meanwhile, he had kept his purity, praying that God would give him a virgin wife. When he learned of his fiancee's past, he cried, Elisabeth said, for three days.

Elisabeth said that Christians should take their cues on sexual matters from Scripture, instead of the world. Yet, in the church, there is a lack of courage to stand up and be counted and take a firm stand on an unpopular matter. We'd prefer to follow the world's example, which is why evangelical theologian Francis Schaeffer is said to have remarked, "Tell me what the world is saying today and I'll tell you what the church is saying seven years from now."

Presently, lack of sexual activity is viewed as abnormal. How abnormal I didn't know until I met the author of a newsletter, *The Sexual Abstinence News,* written by Jack Burkett, a seismic programmer in his early fifties who lives in Houston. Burkett was ahead of his time by about ten years back in 1976, when he founded the Institute for the Cultural and Scientific Study of Chastity with a white rose as its symbol. He conducted a massive study of chastity with the help of researchers from Houston's Rice University and the University of Texas School of Public Health. He started looking for material on chastity while working as a programmer for the School of Public

Health, but came up with nothing on the subject. But he found volumes in print on human sexuality. Looking further, Burkett discovered that even college students didn't know the meaning of the word; only that singer Cher Bono had a daughter by that name.

He commissioned a 1975 study by Dr. Peter Tobias, a doctoral recipient at Rice at the time, on chastity that took up 425 man hours and hundreds of books and professional journals. Tobias later wrote in the study, "In my professional opinion, very little scientific work has been done or reported relating to abstinence, bachelorhood, celibacy, chastity, continence, spinsterhood, or virginity. . . . In many of the more recent studies chastity, etc., has assumed the same 'outcaste' position that sex held at the time of earlier studies (in the late 1800s or early 1900s)."

Jack Burkett proved to be for me a gold mine on this rarely researched area. Although his foundation folded for lack of interest, the coming of AIDS has piqued people's curiosity anew. His newsletter has subheadings like, "Abstainers Don't Have to Explain Themselves" and "Should Closet Abstainers Come Out?" With the first topic, he gives a perfect comeback to the are-you-having-a-relationship-with-anyone-these-days query with a cool reply like, "Sexual abstinence is my sexual preference. It is the way I want to behave sexually."

He also writes tongue-in-cheek about "chastiphobia," an irrational fear experienced by persons afraid of what would happen to them were they to abstain from sex. Burkett's sarcastic note in one newsletter runs thus: "Chastiphobics can be extremely wild-eyed. They believe abstainers reproduce themselves and where they associate with the young, the young will start abstaining too until they are everywhere. One thought is that if sexual abstinence was normalized, there might not be enough people born and the entire human race would perish."

He has horror stories to tell of professionals in the medical and psychiatric professions who thought that abstinence ought to be put in the psychiatric "illness model," much like homosexuality was before 1973 when the American Psychiatric Association voted to remove it from its list of illnesses. Burkett's researchers turned up examples of professional counselors who had strong biases against chastity, considering it to be unhealthy. Some of the lesser-trained counselors, they reported, found chastity a topic "too foreign to be imagined," and also felt that all therapy should be aimed at increasing sexual expression. To them, sex was a biological necessity. Some of the scientists interviewed felt that chastity stood for a non-behavior and that scientific inquiry must deal with observable phenomena. That comes as a surprise to those of us who practice chastity, no doubt, to learn that our lifestyle is a "non-behavior." How absurd, Jack and I agreed, that portions of the professional community consider our lifestyle as deviant. It is more acceptable to talk about AIDS than abstinence.

Whereas I had gone the religious route in promoting chastity, Jack has taken the sociological route. The going, he says, is rough. When one researcher interviewed a group of social scientists, she found that some were repulsed by the term "chastity." Overall, the social scientists had such negative reactions against that word that she suggested that future research projects on the matter choose another word. First, she wrote, some respondents felt the term was old-fashioned, outdated, and quaint. Others felt the term was antiquated. Some of the women felt the word was sexist, referring only to women. Still others felt the word carried value judgments with it and many associated the term with suppression and repression. Now that widespread sexual disease has brought the word "chastity" back into vogue, people are bound to have similar reactions.

"The situation hasn't changed," Burkett told me over lunch one day. "Abstinence isn't mentioned any more in public schools. All they want to tell everyone about is condoms and safe sex." And like me, he found religious leaders of little help in promoting abstinence.

"This universe is not arranged so that a sexual experience is the supreme experience of love," he said. "If anything gets young people to want sexual intercourse, it's to have a religious leader describe what a mystical experience it is. Still, sexual abstinence has become a religious issue, not a scientific or a medical one. That's why doctors can't really discuss it; they have no scientific or medical information about it. You don't notice doctors handing out booklets on sexual abstinence in their offices, do you?"

No, not really, and certainly not on my turf, the media. Last year, I chanced on a story on the Knight-Ridder newswire that reviewed Gordon Thomas's new book on celibacy, *Desire and Denial*. Thomas called the celibacy practiced by Catholic religious orders a "life against nature" that caused sexual difficulties among every one of the 167 religious he interviewed. There were plenty of damning examples of frustrated nuns and priests who lived in their own worlds of sexual fantasy plus statistics on the large numbers of priests and nuns who have left their orders over the celibacy issue. I don't argue against celibacy being difficult. It seems that many of these people bought into celibacy along with their call to the religious life because celibacy was part of the package. But now, with the culture so against them, they found they had no personal convictions on the matter and so chose to leave. But I disagree that celibacy and attendant virtues are "against nature."

Ann Landers ran a recent column from a male virgin who termed himself "Socially Retarded in Flushing." He got a sarcastic reply from someone who wrote, "You are not socially retarded. You are socially confused. In today's world, where using people for sex appears to be normal, the opposite is true. Instead of kicking yourself because you have never kissed a girl nor had intimate relations, count yourself lucky that you have never used a person as a sex machine, never exposed yourself to venereal disease and, most important, you have not broken God's law. Instead of looking for someone to shack up with, look for a friend. You will end up much happier than the guy who has bedded down hundreds of women and is now wondering about the state of his health."

That sort of man is like many of us: unwilling celibates whose call to a holy life outdoes the call of our glands. Although not called to lifelong celibacy, many of us are living that lifestyle for an indeterminate time. While perpetual singleness or perpetual virginity has never been dealt with at any singles seminar I've heard of, our secular culture trashes virginity. Someone passed me a page from some general circulation magazine that ran an article titled, "Virgins: Do Men Secretly Prefer Them?" (Notice, not "Virgins: Do Women Secretly Prefer Them?" which means that such magazines can't imagine men as virgins.) About one-third of the men polled said yes. They were the ones who said that virgins guaranteed them against catching sexual disease or could be molded to their style of lovemaking. Again, I noticed little concern on the part of the men about keeping themselves pure so *their* partner could avoid sexual disease.

I remember an episode during a health education class in high school when the teacher asked the female students how many of them wanted their husbands to be virgins. I was the only girl who raised her hand for several seconds until one of my friends, seeing me, raised her hand also. Elisabeth Elliot in *Passion and Purity* writes that back in the 1950s, she chose to look for a husband who prized his virginity. And she got a prize of a husband, too. "It is possible to love passionately and stay out of bed," she writes. "I know. We did it. . . . There is dullness, monotony, sheer boredom in all of life when virginity and purity are no longer protected and prized. By trying to get fulfillment everywhere, we get it nowhere."

However, Elisabeth didn't just fall into this match. She took to heart the scriptural admonition that her body was not her own. In her early teens she decided never to kiss or hold hands with anybody but the man she would marry. Now she says that all teenagers who want to stay virgins until marriage must make a decision early in life between them and God, admitting that God is their master and that they will rein in their sex lives for his sake. While making this commitment to holiness and purity, they must understand that God isn't out to spoil their fun, she adds. Rather, if they practice self-control now, they get joy, fulfillment, and bliss later. Anyone who hasn't made this decision by high school graduation had better make it before their first all-campus beer party during college freshman orientation. How well I remember my first such party. I had no choice as to whether I wanted to be part of it or not; it was all around me. As I had nowhere off campus to go, I stayed there, seemingly one of the few people there that night who wasn't out to get drunk or end up in bed.

Elisabeth's views on physical affection sound conservative, but I was immensely relieved to hear them. I thought I was one of the few women left in the world who feels uncomfortable kissing a man towards whom I feel indifferent. I have always felt I would be leading such men on, promising what I never intend to deliver. Elisabeth summarized my feelings when she said that certain gestures and ways of expressing oneself are appropriate to an engagement situation but inappropriate to friendship or even serious relationships. I've long had the gut feeling that all but the most social of gestures should be reserved for the man I mean to marry. The problem is not that we spoil sex by taking it too seriously; actually, we dilute and poison it because we don't take it seriously enough.

Take, for instance, the transition from virginity to sexual experience. This is smudged and glossed over in modern literature but nearly everyone I've talked with on this matter remembers the first time they had sex and who they had it with. The real truth, writes Tim Stafford in a *Christianity Today* article titled "Intimacy: Our Latest Sexual Fantasy," is that previous Western culture, he wrote, "treated the move from virginity to experience as a change in a person's very being and (Nathaniel) Hawthorne was not far off in printing a scarlet letter into Hester Prynne's skin—so deeply was sex supposed to influence a person . . . when people lose their virginity, they are affected. Their view of the future changes. If they once imagined themselves as sleeping only with the love of their life, they now usually must adjust to the reality that they will have many sexual partners."

Granted that sex represents the most vital and intense sensual experience of which the body is capable and that sexual surrender involves a subordination to the other, who are we to do it so casually? We are laying bare our souls as well as our bodies. A friend of mine who operates a farm once wrote me about the advantages of virginity because, "What you bring to a relationship is simplicity," he said. "To a greater extent than most people today, you are not encumbered by the excess baggage of fouled-up relationships and wrong-headed affairs that from God's view, should never have happened. Often it occurs to me that what drags down so many relationships is that the two people have too much history to deal with. Again and again, spectres rise up out of the past and blight it. Too many people have been down the same road too many times. It will be so much easier for you because you have not gone the wrong way. You can offer yourself without having to bring along a lot of stuff that does not belong."

My friend added that, "In the Bible, God says that when a man and woman have intercourse, the mere act is enough to make them one flesh. When they part after the act, a little piece of the man stays with the woman and a little piece of the woman with the man. Now in marriage, this is of course alright. But in the case of a one night stand, it is ultimately disastrous. Each partner is stuck for life (and eternity as well?) with a bit of person whom he doesn't want but can't get rid of. Eventually after a hundred or two one-night stands, he is missing a lot of him that he needs and dragging around a lot of fragments of people he would dearly love to get rid of. Does this sound like the situation in which some of the people you have known have found themselves?"

Sure does. Sex belongs in a special manner to God and he's reserved for it a special sphere. This concept is radically different from how sex is portrayed today. Sexual purity is squandered as a matter of routine among my generation, a sexually scarred generation if there ever was one. It's a shame that many people never understood the bonding nature of sex before they experienced it. Because the partners are at a place where they can reveal their most intimate and delicate sides to each other, having sex with someone outside of marriage is a desecration of the act of sex. Then again, much of late twentieth century Western culture is a desecration of things once so meaningful: families, good literature, music, and education are examples. Small wonder that sex reigns chief among those things desecrated.

It has not always been this way. A theology or ethic of virginity helped keep the standard of sexual purity high for hundreds of years primarily through the Roman Catholic church because of its stand on celibacy for priests. Dating back to several hundred years after Christ and lasting to the present, virginity has been seen as union with God. That is, virgins forsook genital sexuality to be single for Christ. Not being caught up in a human relationship meant more time for the divine relationship. Thus, virginity was as valid a lifestyle as marriage.

As the guardian of culture and morals during the Dark and Middle Ages, the Catholic church made virginity an easier goal than sex. Sexual relations were forbidden during Advent, Lent, on Sundays, Wednesdays, and Fridays, before receiving communion, and on Ember Days. Later, for religious reasons, sex was also forbidden on Mondays, Thursdays, and Saturdays.

During the eleventh century there was the cult of the Virgin Mary, in whose honor cathedrals were built all over Europe. It should be said that most female saints were virgins, a lesson not lost on women of the Middle Ages and Renaissance. Women had only one outlet other than marriage and motherhood: to remain a virgin and enter a religious order. This was supported in Christianity until the Reformation and even then, Calvin said virginity was a higher vocation than marriage.

This attitude toward virginity contrasts with the Old Testament view, where virginity, especially for men, wasn't emphasized much, except in the story of Joseph and Potiphar's wife. Old Testament Hebrew has no word for "bachelor." Both the stories of Jephthah's unfortunate virgin daughter in Judges 11 and the anxiety of matriarchs Sarah, Rachel, and Hannah over their childlessness plus biblical instructions on levirate marriage in order to secure descendants for a deceased relative are indications of Israelite predispositions toward marriage and fertility. Singleness was not a sought-after lifestyle and celibacy was almost unheard of for the Jew. Not even the Nazirites, that special class of consecrated people described in Numbers 6, were celibate.

The Christians didn't lift up the ideal until the midpoint of the third century, out of reverence for Christ's virginity. Celibacy carried with it the Stoic idea that sex was tainted and a concession to the weakness of the flesh. Celibacy wasn't considered to be apostolic in origin, but its popularity caught on early. St. Justin (circa 165) and other apologists pointed to the large number of Christians living celibate lives as proof of the high moral quality of Christianity. Male and female celibates, who lived with their families, enjoyed great esteem in the Christian community and pretty soon, the term "brides of Christ" began to be applied to them. As a theological basis for this exalted position, the virginal life of total self-sacrifice was declared by the church fathers to be the worthiest substitute for death by martyrdom, especially as the number of martyrs decreased. Tertullian, a second century theologian living in Carthage, referred to this as "marrying only God." By the middle of the third century, Origen, a theologian born in Alexandria, held up celibate clergy as the ideal.

The ensuing battle over getting the clergy to comply with this idea took well over one thousand years to completely enforce. Their reasons dated back to the Old Testament example of David, when he asked the priest Ahimelech for bread in 1 Samuel 21:4. The priest would only give out the bread provided that the men had "kept themselves from women." Here was one instance where sex was seen as a profane activity, and those who abstained from it were set apart for the service to the sacred. As time went on, restrictions were tightened. St. Cyril of Jerusalem requested sexual abstinence for the clergy before celebrating Mass in the mid-fourth century. Pope Siricius in the late fourth century was the first pope to set out conjugal guidelines for the clergy of the Western church that said they must either be virgins or, if converted as adults, pledge perpetual abstinence. These guidelines were both followed and flouted. The reasoning for abstaining from sex while married came from 1 Corinthians 7:5 which urges Christians to abstain from sex while devoting themselves to prayer. This was applied to priests, because they were supposed to be continually in prayer and thus continually celibate. If Paul instructed the laity to abstain from their wives temporarily for the sake of prayer, how much more should priests whose permanent service is one of prayer and sacrifice abstain at all times, so the logic went. Bishops, priests, and deacons who gathered in council in Carthage in A.D. 390 agreed that they must avoid intercourse with their wives because all of them touched the altar or the sacraments. Since the bread and wine was considered to be the body and blood of Christ and because Christ was born of a virgin, those Christians assumed that Christ required the priest to be a virgin and not married.

The evolution of priestly celibacy, although fascinating, is beyond the scope of this book. But it shows us how early Christians came to view sex. Note that Christianity always upheld the sanctity of marriage; it was heresies like Manichaeism in the fourth century that disparaged marriage and advocated abstinence because sex bound man to matter, which was supposed to be evil.

What a reversal of roles virgins find themselves in so many centuries later! Twenty years ago, the virgin was "on the same team with crew cuts and sensible orthopedic shoes and Billy Graham and the Republican Party," wrote Joyce Maynard, author of *Looking Back: A Chronicle of Growing Up Old in the Sixties*. Virgins were those people whose only pills were vitamins and aspirin. In September, 1970, the Vatican revived a shortened version of the ancient rite of virginal consecration that enabled Catholic women to take a public vow of virginity while remaining in secular society. The Sacred Congregation for Divine Worship, which made the announcement, said the new rite was "a mark of esteem for women whose dignity is sometimes offended in our society, which is often dominated by vulgar hedonism." But, "Few women are expected to take the vows," said a Vatican official quoted in *Time* magazine. *Commonweal* magazine criticized the Catholic church for reviving a concept that it considered was a throwback to the Middle Ages.

But the concept may be flowering again, among Protestants, even. In the summer of 1979, I was visiting and writing an article on Reba Place Fellowship, a Mennonite covenant community in Evanston, Illinois, where I met a few single women. The first time I ever heard of the concept of "living single for the Lord"—the twentieth century version of consecrated virginity—was when a stunning, willowy blonde woman in her early twenties gave me a tour of the community households. As we were chatting, she dropped the bomb that she was thinking of remaining perpetually single to better serve Christ. I was floored. This lady would've drawn a crowd on any college campus in a few minutes time. What a waste, I thought to myself. She looked at me, gauging my guarded reaction. "Only in community," she said finally, "could you consider such a thing."

She had a point there. Having given up sexual intimacy with a husband, she would have to rely on spiritual intimacy with her brothers and sisters in Christ. My ideas of perpetual virgin types were always people who looked fat and dumpy and were at least forty. Actually, it is people like this woman at Reba Place who, by remaining virgins, can capture the imagination of the secular world and do more to spread the gospel than one thousand tracts. These people, who have turned their backs on the twentieth century god of sex, draw awe from most observers, particularly if they are young, attractive, and well able to be sexually active if they so chose. Sex is so central to most of humanity that choosing virginity does mean dying to this world. Sexual abstinence could be the new radicalism of the '90s, since giving up money or lovely homes for God is passé. It's the pouring-out-the-expensive-perfume-on-the-feet-of-Jesus idea; the spectacle of extravagantly wasting what to this generation is more sought after than perfume.

When James Dobson asked Elisabeth Elliot how the single Christian could reconcile his or her desire for sex and marriage with the absence of a mate, she urged all virgins, young and old, to be confident that God will satisfy them. She cautioned us not to listen to Satan questioning us as he questioned Eve with, "Is that what God said? Is that really what God wants for you?" as he tries to trap us into believing that God doesn't really care for us. She pointed out that she was widowed from age twenty-nine to her second marriage at age forty-two, the time of a woman's sexual peak, yet God comforted and satisfied her.

Chastity is the way of the cross for many of us. But there is power in the cross of Christ. We must be willing to lose our lives, to give up sexual satisfaction for the sake of Jesus Christ because after all, he did it for us.

Celibacy may be a lifestyle many of us end up living out of default, but what sort of spiritual power might be unleashed if a group of people ardently desired it? I got to visit such a group of people in June 1987 when I spent three days with The Word of God, an ecumenical Christian community spread throughout Washtenaw County west of Detroit and centered in Ann Arbor's leafy precincts. The Word of God has a corps of celibate men and women known as The Servants of the Word ("the brotherhood") and The Servants of God's Love ("the sisterhood"). After sitting in during an hour-long worship session with some of the men in the brotherhood, I understood what makes them tick: worship. They have a lively, adoring quality to their worship. Their prayers are an expression of their intimacy with God.

I talked with more than ten members of the brotherhood and sisterhood and each of them told me that their ability to worship God stemmed from their experience of being "baptized in the Holy Spirit," an empowering experience mentioned in the New Testament. It was this experience that radicalized them and provided a pivotal point in their decision to join The Word of God. "A lot of us appreciate the charismatic mode of prayer because it is expressive," said brotherhood member Paul Beckman. "It takes you out of being self-focused, which is helpful when you are single."

The brotherhood numbers one hundred men; the sisterhood numbers twenty women. They range from age 26 to 47. Most made their lifelong decisions to stay "single for the Lord," as they term it, in their twenties. The spirituality in this community is light years beyond what I've observed in most Christian groups which may be why, in an age when religious vocations are taking a nose dive, this community is bringing them in at record pace. Newcomers are accepted for a one-to-two-year trial period during which they try out the celibate life.

The brotherhood was founded in 1971 by five men who wished to follow the 1 Corinthians 7 dictate that a single man or woman has more time for the Lord. These men decided to forego marriage and family for the option of spreading the gospel and so drew up a covenant, which in its latest revised form numbers 23 single-spaced typewritten pages full of biblical references. The sisterhood convenant is similar, although worded to reflect a more feminine outlook.

Before being considered for membership in the brotherhood and sisterhood, candidates must belong to The Word of God or one of a dozen sister communities in The Sword of the Spirit, a worldwide network of Christian communities. If accepted, one is invited to become an associate for an open-ended time, usually one or two years. Many of these people stay. The next step is to become an associate in training for three or four years to discern if this is God's call on their lives. After several years of living the life, men and women make lifelong commitments to remain single for the sake of loving and serving the Lord and his people.

"If you treat marriage as an unbreakable bond, you treat singleness in the same way," Paul Beckman said. "Parents ask us, 'What if you find a nice girl? What if things change?' I tell them they didn't leave their mates because they saw other options. This is a serious commitment to God."

Newer brotherhood members say they were attracted to the easy masculinity they saw among the older men. Stuart Ferguson, the son of a forester and a veteran of five years working on a mineral drilling rig, had a distaste for the effeminate. "Many Christian men I had (previously) met seemed too sweet for my taste," he said. "But these (in the brotherhood) were strong guys, guys I could relate to." He ended his relationship with a girlfriend and connected himself with The Word of God.

Many factors make this lifestyle work: a commitment to simplicity as all of them have everything in common; fasting once a week; daily prayer, worship, and Bible study; and weekly meetings in small support groups.

I doubt whether the brotherhood or the sisterhood could survive without the support and acceptance of the other 2,900 members of The Word of God, nor do I believe that The Word of God would be what it is today were it not for this corps of men and women. The celibate lifestyle is possible with the components I found in Ann Arbor: worship, baptism in the

Holy Spirit, a sense of sacrificial calling, a personal challenge from the Lord, a solid relationship with him, a covenant or formal agreement to celibate and shared lives together, a lengthy period of testing that calling, an intent to take celibacy with as much seriousness as one takes marriage, a disciplined lifestyle, a strong emphasis on developing one's femininity and masculinity, a missions outreach, and a commitment to chastity and simplicity. Not all these factors could be duplicated everywhere but they do serve as signposts to remind the rest of us what is possible.

Intimacy with Christ

THE SUMMER OF 1987 WAS a rat race for me. While writing this book and preparing for Pope John Paul's United States visit that September (a major event for any religion reporter since such visits come about once a decade), my co-religion writer left for another paper. So there I was, barely ten months into the job, having to fill one of the country's largest weekly religion sections in a daily newspaper while covering breaking religion news and writing articles on the papal visit. The latter was especially significant for us since one of the papal stops was in Texas. It was a job for three people.

As I saw my job swell to over fifty hours a week, one of the things that suffered was my times alone with God. My Bible study times went by the wayside. As Bible study tends to feed and nourish our times with the Lord, I noticed myself getting more and more drained, as I was having to give out a lot without taking much in spiritually. It's not that I didn't ever study the Bible or pray, but I had to reduce these times greatly. It struck me as ironic that at a time when I was writing about intimacy with Christ, in reality I was not able to draw close to him. Fortunately, he understood my circumstances and my heart, and one day in the midst of my busyness, he spoke an endearment to me. This stopped me short and made me realize how much he cared and understood.

The Lord can compensate us for what we lack from people. Recently, a Christian friend from college days called to discuss my book and tell me about her upcoming wedding. Her long wait was almost over, she said; self-control was easier now that she could see the light at the end of the tunnel. But what, she asked, was I going to tell all those people who weren't getting married soon—if ever? I told her I had decided to describe the great value of spiritual intimacy with Christ. "It seems to me," I said, "that sex often doesn't produce more than fleeting intimacy and sometimes not even that." My friend agreed. It helped having close friends, I said, namely brothers and sisters in Christ. Yet, people fail us and often intimacy just isn't available from them, especially at night. And so we are driven to Jesus, the only one who can give us the intimacy we long for.

"God doesn't have favorites, but he does have intimates," writes Kenneth Swanson, an Episcopal priest whose 1987 book *Uncommon Prayer: Approaching Intimacy With God* stresses that ordinary people can become very intimate with God. But like with all relationships, this one demands a lot of time. It doesn't come instantly. First, we need to listen and feel comfortable with him, an element I missed so badly that busy summer when I didn't have the time to listen. One thing we can do as we linger in God's presence is to behold the love between the Father and the Son in the heavenly places. It helps to set aside time, at least five minutes a day, merely to behold the Lord. What tends to happen is that when we become truly silent, the things we've repressed come out. When we draw close to God's love, we can call our struggles by name and hand them over to God. As we continue this spiritual gazing at the Lord, we are changed from glory to glory. It helps to express this somehow, such as praising the Lord and assuring him of our love for him as we fall asleep at night and wake in the morning.

We often don't dare to be intimate with our God because he demands obedience and discipline. We don't even want to consider his demands for staying pure. We don't want to give up our access to sex because we don't trust God to satisfy our sexual desires. We may think he is capable of doing anything—

but not that. But he can, through spiritual intimacy. God is the only one who can fully satisfy our natural desire for intimacy, and once we allow him to do that, the sexual desires are easier to control. They don't disappear but they do become manageable.

As we tell the Lord we are willing to obey him in sexual matters, he will show us certain conditions to meet. These include:

—**Coming out from behind our walls:** Robert Faricy in his book *Seeking Jesus in Contemplation and Discernment* suggests approaching God in a childlike—not childish—way. "Psychologists have determined that the appropriate behavior for an adult in an intimate love relationship is childlike behavior," he wrote.

Children have few if any pretenses. They are candid about their thoughts and feelings. This insight helped me greatly when I first read it during a vacation in Quito, Ecuador. I couldn't communicate much with the people there because of my poor Spanish so I had time to think about this while gazing at the mountains surrounding the city. I realized I didn't have to act toward God like I would during an interview: poised in a chair with pen in hand. Prostrate on the floor might be more appropriate of my true condition before God. Or kneeling. Or dancing. How does a child act? Children rarely keep still so why should I? I found it healthy to express emotions during prayer times since there is a difference between emotions and emotionalism. The first is real, the second is staged. This can be awkward at first, as vulnerability takes work. Also, it is okay to be insistent with him as a child can be with a parent. It is okay to demand, to take liberties with him, to cease from this horrible spiritual formality we too easily slip into. How many children calmly ask us for lemonade or popcorn? Usually, they're bouncing up and down with excitement and impatience. We don't have to calmly inform him of our sexual needs, either. Dutiful prayers get tepid answers. On such matters, I am blunt and insistent when I pray and instead of being insulted, the

Lord gives clear answers. And not in Elizabethan English, either. God enjoys impassioned prayers.

—**Confessing sin:** Just as we like to be showered and scented before greeting guests, so we need a spiritual bath before spending time with the Lord. I sometimes forget that intimacy needs to be a pleasure to him, too. I find that unforgiveness blocks intimacy and if I refuse to forgive a certain person, he just withdraws until I give in. I find that he has no patience for my complaining about other people. As for other sins, things always look bigger in the dark. Bringing them into the light and showing them to the Lord helps immensely. I find the light of his scrutiny cleansing rather than painful, especially when I detect great kindness behind it. But he needs our permission to deal with these things.

Someone once compared the temptations of the devil to a girl being sexually abused by a stranger. What father wouldn't deliver her from that? And no one would ever say it was the child's fault. But the important thing is to get that child freed as fast as possible from that clinging evil. The evil must be brought into the light where it can be commanded to leave and its victim dealt with lovingly. It's much more difficult for God to reach us while we hide in the closet of our sins or fears. Whenever I've confessed sin, I've never gotten rebuffed by God. It seems like the more penitent we are, the gentler he is. Even if we don't feel very penitent, what matters is our intent and the words we tell him. He can change our feelings. What he hates is pride that won't bow down and confess. Jesus lovingly received the penitent such as the woman in Luke 7:37 who washed his feet with her hair while his host looked on with contempt. The dinner host couldn't see beyond the fact that she was an "immoral woman," probably a prostitute, until Jesus compared her lavish repentance with the host's stingy hospitality. Jesus was impressed by her unmistakable contrition. When it comes to dealing with God, I suggest we throw away our pride.

—**Humility:** Often kneeling as we pray is helpful. The position of the body isn't necessary to salvation, of course, but it certainly puts us in the right frame of mind. It is humbling to love and the proud person, who cannot love, cannot grow. This attitude is essential to unveiling ourselves before the Lord. More often, our reaction is self-hate, but 1 Peter 5:6 suggests that humility is the best way to approach him.

—**Trust:** It's taken me years to realize the Lord isn't out to let me down. When we survive a harrowing experience, such as a near car accident or almost getting fired from a job, and we know that only his mercy kept us safe, this builds trust. We begin to believe he won't let us down. We honor God by doing this and we insult him when we doubt his love, help, and power. "But, without faith," says Hebrews 11:6, "it is impossible to please him, for he [or she] who comes to God must believe that he is and that he is a rewarder of those who seek him." (NAS)

Sometimes trust is built on less than spiritual matters. I can't begin to list the times I've been stuck on a news story with the deadline drawing near and mysteriously I've been bailed out. I remember once while covering the city of Miramar, which is about ten miles northwest of Miami, I was told by an editor to drive to Miramar (which was several miles from the office), find a number of police officers, interview them about their contract negotiations, and be back in the office in about two hours. I panicked. How on earth was I going to find police officers short of breaking every speed limit in town? "Lord, only you can get me out of this one," I prayed fervently. I raced to this small city and saw a patrol car driven by one of the few officers I knew. He radioed to some of his friends on the force and within ten minutes I was surrounded by talkative officers with all the quotes I needed. My trust in God took a leap upward after that. God had come through when I most needed him.

—**Contemplation:** In growing closer to the Lord, author Henri Nouwen suggests silence, studying, and meditating on the Bible, and seeking spiritual direction. A spiritual director needs to be a person we can trust deeply since we're letting them view an intimate part of our lives with God. Spiritual direction is good insurance against going spiritually awry. I've found a spiritual director to be a great person to bounce things against to see if I am perceiving things right. This person needs to be a good listener, someone who knows the Lord intimately, and someone who cares for you. In Florida, I had a male spiritual director with whom I met once every two months and an older female friend with whom I met weekly to discuss more female-oriented concerns, including sexuality and sexual temptations. I'd never suggest discussing sexual matters with a male counselor unless his wife is in the same room. Without a woman present, the hazards for sin are too great. Spiritual direction is a good way to stay spiritually balanced, and a good spiritual director is a real treasure. I committed myself to seek spiritual direction about six or seven times a year and I stuck with that commitment. I didn't feel like keeping my appointments many times, but it was often those "off" times, when I couldn't discern anything happening inside, that yielded the most insightful sessions.

—**Vulnerability:** I once thought I had to manufacture love for God. It took me years before I felt much positive emotion for him. What turned the tide was being honest and vulnerable enough to admit that I really didn't love him. Once we had faced this reality together, our relationship began to blossom. It took many years to work myself out of thousands of "oughts" and "shoulds" in our relationship to a point where I didn't grieve him not because the Bible forbade me to sin but because I cared for him.

I've learned to spend time with him, hearing his opinions on a matter. I've found that if I treat God like a person, I get a personal reply. How do I know I'm not making all this up? By the kind of replies I get to questions I ask him; the kind of discerning replies that I know I could not have thought up myself. It is this relationship that I cling to when sexually tempted. Whereas beforehand I had rejected sexual involvements because I knew they were wrong, I now turn them down for the additional reason that to disobey God would hurt him terribly. Our relationship changed from a legalistic obey-me-or-I'll-kill-you sense I had from God to obey-me-because-I-love-you. My being honest with him—and his acceptance of that honesty—changed my perceptions of him. And as I have made myself vulnerable to Him, he has made himself vulnerable to me. God entrusts himself to us.

Isn't this true of the best human relationships? We hurt the ones we're closest to the most. When we perceive God as being vulnerable, he is easier to love. We feel most for the person we choose to—or not to—hurt. We find that our strength is in vulnerability. We put up walls to protect us, but they keep people—and often God—out. Who wants to approach a fortress? God so desires our love that often he'll take the initiative to give us things merely to please us. What an awesome thought: the king of the universe wants to please us.

—Cost: Intimacy builds in a relationship when we pay dearly for it. Time in prayer, time in fasting, time in showing up for house church, Bible study, early morning prayer. Once during college, I remember hearing a speaker say that intimacy with God was what made him leave the lunch line at the college cafeteria and go off to pray. Once he was standing in a cafeteria line, salivating over the spaghetti—one of the few decent items the cafeteria had to offer—on that day's menu when he sensed a yearning from God that was drawing him to pray instead of eat. "Lord," he said, "are you really worth more than that spaghetti?" He missed his lunch, but gained a deeper relationship with his Lord that day.

—Surrender: Sex involves a complete surrender of our bodies to another person. When we can't have that physical surrender, it's particularly important to yield on a spiritual level. This is why I regularly pray in tongues. It took me years before I saw much use in this gift of the Holy Spirit. I eventually realized that as I surrendered my intellect by praying in this inarticulate fashion, my ability to love and worship the

Lord grew. Doubtless I had been letting my spirit express love to him as I worshipped. We can express the inexpressible and speak tenderly to God in this fashion.

Surrender is the key to letting God effectively fulfill our longings for sex. I better understood this truth while on a trip to Israel where I found a book by Mother Basilea Schlink, the founder of the Evangelical Sisters of Mary from Darmstadt, West Germany. They have a branch house on the Mount of Olives in Jerusalem. It is a lovely house surrounded by flower beds and it is where I found *My All for Him*. What a radical little book. I spent a few days alone at a convent in the Old City, meditating and thinking on this book in which Schlink described "bridal love," a sort of all-encompassing love of Christ, where we desire only to be loved by him. She gives insight on how to be undivided about Christ: how to undertake unglamorous tasks for him, how to think about him until you feel compelled to worship him constantly.

I had supposed such devotion was impossible for those of us who commute to work, do the laundry, and occasionally overdraw our checking accounts. But I decided to inform God that I henceforth would trust him utterly in terms of marriage and sex. I placed my sexual future in his hands. It was the most precious thing I could turn over to him and it was a risk, but if I didn't, I knew our relationship would stagnate. So I went for broke. I laid everything on the altar and waited for an answer.

His response was a most gracious, tender answer to prayer. He didn't remove any of the desires, but he gave me more power to say no to them. In surrendering them to him, I paradoxically got them back in a redeemed form. In other words, he wasn't out to de-sex or make a female eunuch out of me, but to give me a greater ability to bring my thoughts out in the light and discuss them with him. I found that he was less concerned with their content than he was in my willingness to surrender them to him. He wanted to be part of my pain. In surrender, I was admitting them and placing them in his hands to do with as he wanted.

When we give God control of our sexual lives, he gives us greater control. He also demands obedience. Often he'll give us a blunt assessment of what he thinks of us. This gets very personal. One impression I got was delight from him over virginity. Like, he really appreciated it. He knew the sacrifice it entailed. No one had ever told me this before. No one had seemed to care. Just before then, I'd been having these oh-what-is-the-use feelings about it. The Lord, however, seemed so honored that I would trust him on these matters and in return he showed me how vulnerable he had been on this earth and continues to be, as long as he stays involved with his people. I reminded him that I could reject him too. "But you won't," he replied. He trusted me. Intimacy is based on trust that your confidant will not hurt you.

I asked to see the gentleness of God and I got an exclusive love. It was clear that he wanted me for himself. Amazed at this, I brashly promised I'd be exclusively his—for now and forever—if he wished. I wasn't vowing never to marry, but I was promising to forego all kinds of sexual satisfaction until marriage—if I should ever marry. Although I'd always been chaste, I hadn't committed myself to that in so many words. Life with the Lord is made up of many little surrenders and this was one. There was a burning of the bridges here and it meant that should I never get married, I would never experience sex, a frightening thought in our society. In exchange, I received from the Lord the kind of intimacy that went beyond sex and which satisfied. After recounting all this, I told one of my friends that it didn't make any difference any more whether I experienced sex or not whereupon she burst into tears. She admitted that her sexuality was the one area she had never submitted to God because she felt that was the one craving of hers that he couldn't satisfy.

Of course, any resolve will get tested. God is more silent than we would like him to be, and many times I wish I had the constant feedback one ideally gets from a human lover. All our activities really can't hide from us that we do lack physical satisfaction and all our brave beliefs about God get tested in the desert of our long nights. At night, our cheerfulness comes to nothing. What did Jesus do during those times? The few records we have of his times alone: in the Judean desert, early in the mornings and at Gethsemane, he prayed.

I still don't think I possess the gift of celibacy. But I think what I did is possible for any single person who can surrender sexual desires to the Lord and find freedom. And, in seeing Jesus' thirst for love from those he died for, I could offer him the whole of myself instead of half. Paul alluded to this in 1 Corinthians 7 when he said that virgins could be single minded about the Lord. Basilea Schlink is right. Undivided "bridal" love for Christ is possible for any believer.

God is the heavenly lover who wants our souls to cling to him. Sixteenth century writer John Donne compared this to being made a captive of God: "Except you enthrall me, never shall be free/Nor ever chaste except you ravish me." The Lord knows the tenderest of names to call us. But he waits to be involved in our lives. As in a human relationship, he doesn't barge in on intimacies until given permission. As we desire more and more to have God, we discover that God desires to have us and have us perfectly at ease with him.

Dame Julian of Norwich, the famous fourteenth-century English mystic, wrote descriptions of the Lord's personality, such as, "For our courteous Lord will that we be as familiar with him as heart can think or soul desires."

It takes years, I think, to learn to relax with him and to be fully there instead of observing. I get caught in the trap of thinking what the Lord would say in a certain circumstance or how I might respond if he said so and so. What he wants is not that; he wants us to relate to him, not to think about relating to him. So often, we mistake the latter for the former.

God is truly a jealous God. He gets exasperated or jealous when he wants me all for himself and I mentally wander off. I think we should treat our time with Christ with the specialness and privacy that a husband and wife (should) reserve for each other. While worshipping him, I get the impression that he enjoys our time together and is saddened if I cut it off too soon before starting with my petitions for the day.

I've heard friends express frustration over only having a half hour with the Lord because it takes them up to a half hour to quiet themselves down. And then it is time to go to work. Or, if we don't spend time with him during the day, he leaves an emptiness in our souls until we do. Relating to the Lord can be stormy and about as comfortable as a lightning bolt. Once we've given him entrance into our lives, he goes about changing us and eventually, following him does cost us everything we have.

In return, we get eternal rewards. It has been more than fifteen years since I decided to pay that price and believe that God could be trusted to run my life. In the process, my perceptions of him changed from slave master to friend to lover. But I always wanted intimacy. From the beginning, I decided I'd pay whatever it cost me to run the race the whole way, to pass the test, to attain to the high calling of God and to win that intimacy with him that few people invest the time to get. King David made that same decision, so that at the prime of his life he could say, "Thy gentleness makes me great . . . he rescued me because he delighted in me." We can bank our lives on the Lord as David did. The price is high but, if I can paraphrase Revelation 14:3-4, he will give us a song that no one else knows. We will be the first fruits and the pick of his harvest. We will follow the Lamb wherever he goes.